First published in Great Britain in 2009 by Nethergate Writers
Department of Continuing Education
University of Dundee
Nethergate
Dundee, DD1 4HN

All stories, poems and plays © the contributors, 2009
The right of the contributors to be identified as authors of this work has been asserted in accordance with the Copyright, Designs and Patents Act 1988.

Edited by Esther Read
Stories and poems selected by Dr. Jim Stewart
Cover design by Rikki O'Neill. Website: www.RIKOART.co.uk

ISBN: 978-0-9555831-2-4

A CIP catalogue record for this book is available from the British Library

This is a work of fiction. All of the characters, names, incidents, organisations and dialogue in this collection are either the products of the author's imagination or used fictitiously.

Printed and bound in Great Britain by CPI Antony Rowe, Chippenham, Wiltshire

To Rup Annie and Rex

Here's my 'Challenge' hope you enjoy yours and reading it

Love

Jock

Previously published by Nethergate Writers:

Turn Back The Cover (2007)
Roots (2008)

If Stones Could Speak

An anthology of new writing by Nethergate Writers

Edited by Esther Read

Dundee
2009

CONTENTS

Acknowledgements *Ed Thompson*	iii
Introduction *Esther Read*	iv

LOCATION – ANGUS

Blue Skies *Catherine Young*	3
Dilemma *Flora Davidson*	10
The Battle of South Esk *Bob Drysdale*	13
The White Snake of Reekie Linn *Louise Ramsay*	20
Digging In *Jean Langlands*	28

LOCATION – DUNDEE

The Saving O' Murdie Boon *Beth Blackmore*	36
Monkey Tricks *Ann Prescott*	43
Mr. Stanley, I Presume? *Ed Thompson*	50
Right Time, Right Place *Nan Rice*	55
A Walk in the Park *Lesley Holmes*	63
The Winkle Seller *Jane O'Neill*	72
The Ringo Kid *John Mooney*	74
Scratching The Surface *Ward McGaughrin*	80

LOCATION – FIFE

End of the Line *Joyce McKinney*	87
The Bench *George Reid*	94
Through A Glass Darkly *Amanda Barclay*	100
Nora's Garden *Claire MacLeary*	106
Cast Adrift *Stuart Wardrop*	112

The Challenge *Paul Sykes* 117
Vantage Point *Faye Stevenson* 125

LOCATION – PERTHSHIRE

Sinderin *Roddie McKenzie* 135
Release – Glenfarg *Pat Fox* 143
The Stone of the Sidlaws *David Carson* 144

Contributors' Notes 151

ACKNOWLEDGEMENTS

The Nethergate Writers who are the authors of *If Stones Could Speak* are members of Dundee University's extra-mural class, 'Continuing as a Writer' – or rather classes, for its popularity is such that we now have two parallel classes running on different days of the week. We acknowledge with pleasure our many debts of gratitude – first to the Department of Continuing Education for running and supporting the class against a background of severe administrative and financial pressures.

We are grateful once again to artist Rikki O'Neill for designing an outstanding cover for our book, and to Iain Kelman for invaluable advice on typesetting. We owe a special debt to Gordon Dow, manager of the Dundee branch of Waterstone's, for his encouragement and his marketing expertise.

The final selection of submissions for publication was made by Dr Jim Stewart, who teaches Creative Writing in the universities of Dundee and St Andrews; his critique of every writer's work was extremely helpful.

Above all it is Esther Read that we have to thank for the success of the project. As Class Tutor she initiated the *Stones* project at the beginning of the session, and during the next two terms worked tirelessly to get the members of both classes to respond to it, and to find a great deal of enjoyment in the process. She then changed roles and as editor oversaw the intricacies of getting the book into print. The administrative burden was eased by Faye Stevenson (Treasurer) and Jane O'Neill (Secretary), and Flora Davidson and I dusted off old skills to serve as proof-readers, but *If Stones Could Speak* remains a tribute to the enthusiasm and professionalism of our Tutor.

Edward H. Thompson
Chair, Nethergate Writers
2009

INTRODUCTION

Esther Read

Place matters in fiction. It's hard to imagine the story of *Wuthering Heights* set in a city or the events of *Catcher in the Rye* played out in some rural backwater. Characters are who they are, in part, as a result of where they live, while their response to a setting – familiar or not – is often our first point of engagement with them. Place may also provide the theme for a poem or kick-start the plot of a story.

Yet writers first have to explore their own relationship to the setting they have chosen (or which has chosen them). Landscapes, in fiction, are constructed and translated through the senses. Certain aspects will be emphasised, others ignored. No two people will react to the same place in the same way – which is why you may find your own view of familiar landscapes refreshed or transformed by reading this collection.

The stories and poems are grouped together under four geographical headings – Angus, Dundee, Fife and Perthshire. What's striking about the Angus collection is the way in which the beauty of the landscape grips and transforms the characters. In 'Blue Skies' by Catherine Young, the coastal path at St Cyrus offers inspiration in unexpected ways while in 'Dilemma' by Flora Davidson, the wildness of Glen Clova proves a challenge to the rectitude of the character. Meanwhile in 'Digging In' by Jean Langlands, devotion to the country way of life becomes the theme. In 'The Battle of South Esk' by Bob Drysdale, it's the geographical location of Montrose that puts its people at the eye of the storm during the Jacobite rising. A sense of history is interpreted rather differently in 'The White Snake of Reekie Linn' by Louise Ramsay, where there are mysterious forces at work beneath the surface of the landscape.

In the Dundee section of the book, 'The Saving O' Murdie Boon' by Beth Blackmore recreates the hardships of life for two young boys in 19th century Dundee, while a 1950s childhood is realised – though in very different ways – in 'The Winkle Seller' by Jane O'Neill and 'The Ringo Kid' by John Mooney. The settings are, respectively, Broughty Ferry's

Grassy Beach and North Wellington Street, Dundee.

No fewer than three of the writers in this section have chosen to focus on crime in the city. Set in the 1970s, 'Right Time, Right Place' by Nan Rice is an intriguing tale of good old-fashioned detective work which will bring back memories of Dundee at that time. By contrast, 'Scratching The Surface' by Ward McGaughrin, set in The Howff, was described by Jim Stewart, who selected the stories, as 'creepy'. Not so 'Mr Stanley, I Presume?' by Ed Thompson, set in the West End, which proves that even crime can have its light-hearted moments.

Just as unexpected are the events that take place in two of Dundee's more notable beauty spots – the Botanic Gardens and Baxter Park – in 'Monkey Tricks' by Ann Prescott and 'A Walk in the Park' by Lesley Holmes.

Next we move to Fife where the Kingdom is well represented by a very varied collection of stories. Try romance with a modern twist in George Reid's 'The Bench', set in Dunfermline's public park, or golf with a difference in 'The Challenge' by Paul Sykes, the setting being Tarvit House Golf Club, hickory clubs and all. In both 'End of the Line' by Joyce McKinney and 'Nora's Garden' by Claire MacLeary, character and place are effortlessly intertwined – the passing of Elie as a popular seaside resort recorded in the former and the life of St Andrews in the latter.

In the next two stories, setting is emblematic of the inner turmoil of the characters. In 'Vantage Point' by Faye Stevenson, a couple struggle to climb Falkland Hill, a metaphor, perhaps, for the equally insurmountable problems in their relationship. In 'Cast Adrift' by Stuart Wardrop, the character's lack of moral compass is set against the backdrop of North Queensferry at night. The Fife section also offers one of the book's more unusual locations, Methil Power Station, in 'Through A Glass Darkly' by Amanda Barclay, a gripping and eerie story that reflects the importance of the area's industrial past.

In the Perthshire section, it's an agricultural past that is the focus of Roddie McKenzie's moving story, 'Sinderin', while in 'The Stone of the Sidlaws' by David Carson past and present intertwine. In her poem, 'Release – Glenfarg', Pat Fox beautifully encapsulates landscape through sound.

In short, *If Stones Could Speak* is a reflection on the places which shape us and the way in which we in turn, in our imaginations and by our actions, reshape them. It's also a thoroughly good read.

LOCATION – ANGUS

BLUE SKIES

Catherine Young

To her left, the swaying barley, ready for harvest. Long grasses playfully flick against her legs like a wet tea towel. And there's the rustling sound of taffeta skirts from the dressing-up box. It takes a while to locate the noise: wind through dry broom pods. Lots of wind against her face, whipping her hair against her face.

The path curves up and round to the right, following the cliff top. Everything above and to the right is deep azure blue, both the sky and the sea. And smooth. It's all very smooth. She feels enveloped and embraced left, right and above in this beautiful silky hue. "And now, leave your Happy Place for today." The yoga teacher interrupts Anna's thoughts. "Start to stretch. Om shanti shanti shanti. Peace, peace, peace." The buzz of conversation started immediately before she'd even opened her eyes.

Anna hated that crash back into reality. Peace? It was anything but peaceful. The hum of conversation reverberated around the harsh concrete walls. She fondly remembered the polished wooden panelling at the Ward Road Gym, old fashioned even when she was an art student in Dundee. She wondered if it still existed.

She'd been wondering a lot about Scotland recently. The yoga class's Happy Place is what had done it. The cliff top walk at St Cyrus had just popped into her head. She'd only been once in real life but it had made such an impression. She never did find out what was at the base of the cliffs. She'd been so taken with the huge unending blue and massive horizon that she'd forgotten to look down.

"The wind's not allowed to blow on that child's face." It was strange how one snippet of conversation caught her attention, sifted out from all the rest. Her friends, Miranda and Helen, had been on a mission to take her in hand and yoga classes had seemed the best of their offered alternatives. She could certainly do with a bit of inner calm and serenity right now. "So what d'you think Anna?"

"About what?" "Helen was just saying about her Rachel not letting the wind blow…"

"Rachel is being an over-protective parent with that child of hers," Helen butted in.

"It drives us all demented. Anyway you'll see what I mean when you come to ours for Boxing Day. And I'm not taking no for an answer. Can't have you sitting at home all on your own."

Anna threw her sports bag onto the hall floor as soon as she got back to the house. Her old training shoes spilled out and her very expensive metal water bottle clattered and rolled off under the boxes of junk beside the console table. She got onto her knees and fished for it among the overflowing cardboard boxes. It had been her one indulgence.

She sat up on her hands and knees and stretched her right arm forward, reaching for the mail on the mat behind the door. It was surprising how much more supple and flexible she felt after just a few weeks of yoga.

She took one look at the private and confidential envelope – the bank statement for her new account – and quickly put it to the back of the pile. She scrutinised two Christmas cards addressed to 'Mr and Mrs'. Who still didn't know? One was a Barking postcode. "Auntie May!" she fumed. "So I'm supposed to tell *his* bloody auntie." She put that envelope, unopened, to the back as well. The next 'Mr and Mrs' one was from the local garage. Obviously a clerical error. There was no way the tom-tom drums hadn't got that far. Then there was a card addressed to her maiden name. That was somehow worse. Not even her new bank account used that name yet. She put this envelope to the back as well.

The final envelope, from her old art college, looked a little more promising. She couldn't remember getting a Christmas card before so guessed the Alumni Office were using it as an excuse to send round the begging bowl again. She stared at the exquisitely drawn invitation – *Art School Reunion and Exhibition*. Her left hand slowly scrunched the envelope into a tight ball, her knuckles a white bony ridge.

A rattle at the door startled her. "Who's there?"

"Hi Mum. It's me." A black suitcase on wheels was pushed through the half-open front door quickly followed by two large shiny Christmas gift bags, one red and one white.

Anna quickly put the invitation to the back of the pile. "Mhairi, you're early."

"What's happened? Have you fallen?" Mhairi knelt down next to her.

"What? No, I'm fine."

"What're you doing on the hall floor then?'"

"I was just looking for something I dropped."

"What on Earth's all this stuff anyway?"

"Oh it's my broken tiles."

"Yeah, I can see that. What I mean is, Mother, why have you got boxes of broken ceramic tiles under the hall table?"

Anna picked through a box. "Your father wanted to get the bathroom retiled when we put the new shower in. I was all for keeping them. They were beautiful original features. But I came back one day from the office and he'd chiselled them all off. Just like that. No discussion."

"Hmm. Sounds like Dad."

"What? Dumping the old to make way for the new?" She gently rubbed the dust off a small fragment of azure blue ceramic. "Haven't got round to getting rid of them yet. They're such a lovely colour."

Anna reached for the bottle that had rolled under the table. "Found it."

"Ooh, very cool."

"Very indestructible as well, thank goodness. My bag gets thrown to the floor with increasing force every time Miranda and Helen drop me off from yoga class."

"What's the gruesome twosome up to now?"

"They mean well. I just can't help thinking I'm always their main topic of conversation."

"How are you getting on with the yoga anyway? Is it helping?"

"The relaxation bit's good. That's what's got my goat today. The pair of them were chatting when we were supposed to be visualising a walk in our Happy Place."

Mhairi stood up and took Anna by the arm. "C'mon. Time to get up from down here. This floor isn't the comfiest."

BLUE SKIES

Anna picked up the pile of mail. The bank statement was back on top. "Yes, take your coat off and I'll put the kettle on." She looked back at her daughter from the kitchen doorway. "Like the new look by the way. That's not Chanel Red lipstick, is it?'"

"Well spotted," Mhairi yelled from the hall. "Wait till you see the whole ensemble." She posed by the doorframe, "Da-rah!' flicking a long string of huge pearls over a silky white top, black cardigan and red skinny jeans. "'I was fed up being a scruffy student."

"I was the same when I was at art college. I got so messy when I was working that I wanted to make a real effort the rest of the time. And look at me now." She peered at her reflection in the glass oven door. "People from college'd never recognise me. Don't recognise myself some days. When did I become so old and boring?"

"I'm sure you don't look any older than the rest of them."

"But boy do I feel it."

Anna fiddled with a fragment of blue tile, turning it over and over on the pile of mail while her daughter took her bags to her bedroom. She could hear Mhairi chatting on her mobile phone to her friends but also, she realised, to her father. It was going to be an odd Christmas this year, just the two of them at the dining table. Mhairi had emailed at the beginning of November to give her details of a new place to order ethically reared turkey for Christmas dinner, thus cementing the arrangements without anyone having to openly discuss the issue. It appeared she was to get Mhairi up to and including Christmas Dinner then she was off to her father's for the next few days and by the sound of it, New Year was going to be strictly partying with her friends. She was amazed at how Mhairi had taken the lead, bringing 'solutions, not problems', as her final year tutor had frequently snapped at her during her Degree Show. She couldn't remember being quite so grown up as her daughter at twenty.

She took the reunion invitation from the bottom of the pile of mail. On the back of the card was a photo of the woman who had been her best friend all through college, a large painting towering behind her. *Andrea, pictured here with her award-winning 'Self Portrait no-4 in Oils', invites classmates to submit current work for an exhibition to run alongside the reunion celebrations.*

Anna rummaged for the Christmas card addressed to her maiden name. Andrea. Of course. She absently scribbled with the pointed edge of the piece of blue tile, marking out a box around her friend's handwriting on the envelope and then underlining the words. A tiny rip appeared beneath her name. The fragment of blue tile had etched a deep crevice down her fingertip. She rubbed her index finger with her thumb but the fissure remained.

She closed her eyes and breathed. *Breathe in slowly and deeply, breathe out happy and calm. In slowly and deeply, out happy and calm.* The small shard of azure blue ceramic was the exact colour of the sky at St Cyrus. There were acres and acres of blue there. Standing high on the sheer cliffs and looking east, the only thing in vision was the beautiful deep azure of sea and sky. Anything had seemed possible there.

She opened her eyes slowly. Well, she didn't have any artwork, current or otherwise to exhibit and, she decided, she didn't have to go to the reunion. She'd tried her best but had had enough of all the pitying looks and the not knowing what to says. If her soon to be ex could run away from telling even his Auntie May, why should she have to face down a whole roomful of award-winning Andreas?

Anna reached for her watch. three am Boxing Day. There was no point in just lying awake, so she threw off the duvet and got out of bed. She washed up a few glasses and cups then took the vacuum cleaner through to the dining room, though with just the two of them, there wasn't much mess. The hall was a different story though. She could do without Helen scrutinising it when she came to collect her for the forced bonhomie of her family get-together.

Anna shoved the vacuum cleaner back and forth with increasing speed. She didn't want to feel like a spare part in someone else's family. The vacuum crashed into one of the boxes of broken tiles under the table, spilling a few fragments out onto the floor that promptly rattled up the nozzle.

She sat cross-legged on the hall floor shaking the nozzle then peered up it. "Oh, bloody hell," she laughed, throwing it aside. A piece of azure ceramic jingled back down the tube and landed at her feet.

At half past nine she texted Helen from the motorway services just outside Stirling- *Away 2 C old friend in Scotland. Have good party. Anna* – then switched her phone to voicemail and tucked into a huge fry-up. She'd bought a *Scotsman* before she'd gone into the restaurant but no one paid any attention to her:

BLUE SKIES

a woman sitting at her first table for one. In fact there were several people at tables for one. She gazed out the window. It was now a beautiful crisp winter morning. It'd been extraordinary driving at sunrise as the sky gradually brightened. It was imperceptible at first until she finally realised she didn't need to have her headlights on anymore. In a couple of hours she'd be there. At St Cyrus. No need to visualise her *Happy Place*; today she'd be there for real.

She'd remembered the road to the cliffs was next to a coffee shop and found it surprisingly easily. She parked the car and fished around for her digital camera then piled on layers of fleece jackets, hat, scarf and gloves before setting off down the lane. She walked between the church and the primary school buildings, then the graveyard to the left and a grass playing field to the right. Beyond the playing field was rough grass full of molehills. A flock of oystercatchers dipped their beaks in and out of the earth for worms. To the left of this was a field of barley stubble. The lane finally came to an end at a small grassy car park. She hadn't remembered the car park nor the scattering of memorial benches but the start of the path was still as she'd recalled, running alongside the barley field fence.

Anna picked her way over the rabbit holed lacework of turf between the benches and peered over the edge. She hadn't looked down during the first visit all those years ago. She turned, her hair whipping against her face and gazed down and off to her right – south towards Dundee. Below the cliff edge were a few steps then a path coming up the cliff face from a huge wide swathe of sand flats and salt marsh far below. They ran for miles parallel to the sea and the cliffs. There were pathways and little huts (for fishermen's nets, she assumed). There had been a whole different world just out of sight; fishing below, farming above. When she'd pictured St Cyrus she'd always seen it as a huge expanse of blue but here was a large stretch of a beautiful golden colour as well.

A couple walking their dog along the cliff tops stopped to chat and offered to take a photo of her. She'd been taking lots of pictures. She loved the immediacy of digital cameras. The couple recommended a great fish restaurant further up the coast for lunch. At three pm on Boxing Day she was overlooking blue sky and crashing waves, eating amazing Finnan Haddock, sitting at a fabulous window table for one and occasionally sketching on her napkin.

When she got back home Anna spread some of the broken tiles onto the dining-room table, drafting out her mosaic picture. She'd use bold swathes of bright colours. In the left corner, a deep golden triangle: barley ready for harvest; then, a narrow strip of green separating the field from the cliff's edge and a tiny strip of brown path curving up and round to the right, following the cliff top. Above and to the right would be deep blue, both the sky and the sea. She'd need to get some golden coloured tiles for the sand flats – the parallel world running along the cliffs that she'd only just realised was there. But there was plenty of time. Andrea had said in her Christmas card that work could be submitted right up to the week of the reunion.

DILEMMA

Flora Davidson

The smell of pure air penetrates the nasal passages; stimulating and cold, it sharpens the eyes and the understanding. The sound of silence is the rhythm of the blood in the ears. Insistent after the climb and quiet on the summit, it reminds Mind of Body, Brother Ass, which carries Mind about its business. The good beast is occasionally exultant in its youthful health, more often complaining of weariness, and easily placated with a bite to eat. How exquisite the taste of any rubbish in mountain air! Squashed tomatoes washed down with Bass, corned beef in white pan bread – Brother Ass wolfs them rejoicing and bends anew to the load. (I allow myself Bass when alone on the hill. It is rather mannish, but so am I.)

Ah, the load! – OS map and compass, flower book, *British Butterflies* and *The World of Spiders*, geological map, hammer, two specimens of serpentine (weathered and fresh), camera and notebook, primus, small tin kettle, cup and plate, tea and tinned salmon, Zubes and sticking-plaster, and on top of the lot the sleeping bag with waterproof cover, extra pullover, woollen stockings and balaclava. And that's in June.

Brother Ass and I are 2900 feet up on Dun Hillocks among the silvery confetti of a Fleet Air Arm trainer that came down thirteen years ago in Forty-Two. After a quarter of a mile over matgrass, unbeloved by sheep and deer, I must have reached the first outcrop of serpentine, although the rock is entirely covered with black peat. My quarry is the only flowering plant that tolerates serpentine, says the book, but the only plant here is the occasional tussock of matgrass islanded by violent winter run-off. Perhaps Professor Graham and his students filled their vasculums in their day, when the rare botanist plundered the rarer plants. Move on, anyway, to the next possible outcrop half a mile away. There I find more black peat, criss-crossed by the hoof-prints of red deer.

A great herd is below me to the west, above Glen Isla, unaware of human observation as long as no stray air takes them my scent. A Mountain

Flora Davidson

Ringlet flutters over the waste, dissatisfied with the vegetables on offer. I sympathize. The map promises one last outcrop of serpentine between the thighs of Culrannach. Third time - yes, lucky! The alpine catchfly is in bloom!

Grey rock peeps through turf starred with miniature ragged robins. I count ten, twenty naïve pink faces, throw down Ass's load and kneel beside them, ecstatic with the pride of finding something unknown to the general. Lychnis alpina, 'known only high in the Lake District and Angus,' buried in snow for months every year, does not cling for dear life to a shadowed cliff like other rarities but sports in sunshiny turf, presenting its frilly frou-frou above a circlet of leaves. It is a three-star rarity. I want to tell the world, I want to shout, "I've found them!" Instead, I realise I am now the recipient of a secret. Thirty thousand inhabitants of Scotland would like to know, but I won't tell.

As the sun declines I rise, stiff now, and wend downhill along the Fialyach Burn in search of a campsite, down among wood anemones (when was there a wood here? a thousand years ago?) and into the shade of a deep cleft where the infant White Water dallies before its headlong leap into the abyss. Brother Ass is instantly demanding, ravenous. Mind genially unpacks the primus to heat burn water for tea.

What a perfect spot! The burn runs over coloured pebbles between drifts of starry saxifrage. After the harsh plateau this nook is a haven for tall grasses and yellow globe flower. After tea I write up the notebook with today's triumph, then, since it is getting chilly, creep into the sleeping bag. This place, so close to Jock's Road, is perfectly hidden. I have no fear. I sleep like (avoid the cliché – a log? top? dormouse?) Well, I sleep sound anyway and wake in chilly morning shade.

Today I shall do the Dounalt and then work round to Corrie Fee. The sun is already shining almost warmly on the Dounalt rocks. Far below, Jock's Road is empty. No one is up yet. The young have slept at the Youth Hostel and must do a cleaning job before they leave. A pair of peregrine keep up a cry of disapproval as long as they can see me; the moment I am hidden in a gully they forget me. I photograph saxifrages, moss campion, roseroot and a brilliant blue speedwell, but nothing out of the ordinary. I make a note. Northern bedstraw is not yet in bloom.

The birds start shrieking again while I am in the gully. Next

DILEMMA

moment I come face to face with a man. Simultaneously we say "Good morning," then pause. He is dressed in tweed knickerbockers, quite gentlemanly. Both Minds conclude, "It's another botanist."

"Wonderful!" he says, waving a hand round the universe, then, "Found anything special?" and before I can answer, he bursts out, "I got Oxytropis campestris in Corrie Fee! Imagine! A three-star rarity!"

I teeter on the rock. Yellow milk-vetch is 'very rare in Glen Clova and near Loch Loch.' I searched every possible cliff in the Perthshire glen and never found it. As for Glen Clova, that is looking for a needle in a haystack. (I am too moved to seek out an original simile.) Then the silly man spills the beans. (Oh dear, what a common expression. I really can hardly control myself.) He says, straight out, "It's high up on a sort of light-coloured river of rock that comes down just past Craig Rennet."

I try to remain cool. I want to out-boast him with the unique site of a rarity, not just one of two. That is childish. At the same time I want to hurry on to Craig Rennet. That is unethical. I find that Mind is harder to subdue than Brother Ass. At last I offer a poor quid pro quo. "You will find alpine speedwell about fifteen yards on, at this level." He thanks me, lifts his cap and passes on.

I took no more photos on the Dounalt but went on to Corrie Fee and found the milk-vetch. That did not give me the same euphoria as finding the catch-fly. Ridiculously, I felt ashamed of myself. But you know, if he is a member of any botanical society he should know better than divulge the exact position of a rarity. 'In Glen Clova' is close enough, although I must admit it is awfully annoying. (There I go again: 'awfully'!) But surely I was right to keep quiet, wasn't I? Wasn't I? Ethically?

THE BATTLE OF SOUTH ESK

Bob Drysdale

The winter of 1745 was an eventful time for the little port of Montrose. Situated on the East coast of Scotland midway between Edinburgh and Aberdeen and in the centre of an area where Jacobite sympathies were rife, it became the focus for considerable maritime activity. The French privateers who were supplying the Jacobite rebels with arms and men used it frequently. It had a fine sheltered harbour in the form of an inland tidal basin linked to the sea by the mouth of the fast flowing South Esk; and because it could be entered at any time due to the depth of the narrow entrance, it also made a fine refuge from the Royal Navy ships blockading the coast.

One day in mid-November James Cargill, a tobacconist in the town, was out for an afternoon stroll. The day was cold but the south easterly wind was light and the smell of the smoke houses on the Ferryden shore was mingled with the salty tang of the North Sea. James walked down the Coal Wynd towards the harbour, deep in thought. The times were unsettling to be sure, and he had grave misgivings about the events of the past few weeks. He turned to walk along the water side, then glancing up he stopped. Andrew Robertson was standing a few yards away, his back turned, deep in conversation with one of the seamen. He and Andrew had been friends since childhood but there was now an obstacle, which could cause friction, and James had been avoiding meeting him. But it was too late: Andrew had seen him.

After a moment's pause James said firmly, "Good day to you Andra."

Robertson looked at him and frowned. "I had not expected to see your Billy marching out with Ogilvy," he said abruptly.

James sighed. It was out in the open now so he might as well deal with it. His son, William, had enlisted in Ogilvy's regiment the previous month and marched away to join the Jacobite invasion of England.

"His mother and I were as vexed as you, Andra, but when he heard the Auchterlonys had enlisted there was no stopping him."

THE BATTLE OF SOUTH ESK

"Aye, of course, he and Helen Auchterlony were gey close." Andrew Robertson nodded a degree of understanding, then added, "And of coors yon Betty Aucherlony's Faither was oot wi Mar in '15 so she wid be eggin them oan."

"I didna ken that," said James thoughtfully. "They never talked politics when I wis around."

Andrew Robertson sighed. "The way things are Jamie, your lad maybe made richt choice."

James looked at his friend in surprise. Andrew Robertson had never hidden his contempt for the Jacobite cause. "Do you think it is all over then, Andra?"

"Likely not, Jamie, but I fear we will have the devil's ane trouble getting rid of this Stewart now he is back in Edinburgh."

The two men stood in silent thought. Suddenly there was a cry from a man high in the rigging of one of the ships. "Sail ho, a ship heading in!"

"Is it another damned Frenchie?" called Andrew Robertson.

"No, Maister Robertson, she's Navy, a neat little sloop by the look of her."

"Navy by God, at last!" Andrew cried out. "Come on, Jamie, let's welcome the Navy."

With these words he set off at a brisk pace towards the narrow river channel that gave entry to the basin. James Cargill followed hesitantly. With a son now in the service of the rebels he was not sure how he might be viewed by the King's Navy.

It took about half an hour for the small flush-decked warship to make her way into the Montrose basin and drop anchor. In the meantime a considerable crowd had assembled on the waterside and most seemed to be hostile to the new arrivals. James noticed that Mrs Auchterlony and her daughter were to the fore. Andrew Robertson was staring hard at the ship.

"She's *HMS Hazard*, see her name on the bows, and she's ready for trouble."

James, who knew little about such things, realised that the small ship had her guns run out, and a file of red-coated marines stood on deck. "Will she fire on the town?" he asked apprehensively.

"No," said Andrew Robertson, "not unless Scott and his cronies decide to fight." He was referring to the governor and his small band of men who had taken control of the town for the Jacobites.

"Do you think they will?"

"Ha!" snorted Robertson. "They'll probably be halfway to Brechin by now."

It seemed that he was right. While they watched, two boats were lowered from the sloop and a party of sailors and marines landed on the shingle close to the quay. However, although there was no response from the Jacobite Governor the townspeople of Montrose did not appear to be deterred by the military might of the Royal Navy. Indeed the crowd, led by Betty Auchterlony and her daughter, surged forward to face the new arrivals.

"Get back to your King George! We dinna want you here!" she called loudly.

This was echoed by others in the crowd.

A young naval officer stepped forward and held up his hand. "We mean you no harm," he called out. "We are here to re-establish the rightful government of this place."

There was a loud roar of protest at this statement. Then the crowd started to roar out the words to the old Jacobite song:

Who the devil have we got for a king
But a wee bit German lairdie?
When they went to bring him hame,
He was delving in his kale yairdie.

This was followed by more shouts and a few people started to throw stones at the naval party. That was when it began to look ugly. The officer called out an order and the marines formed a line facing the crowd. "You must disperse or we will open fire!" he called out.

The sergeant in command of the marine party called out an order and the marines raised their muskets to point at the crowd. It was at this point that Andrew Robertson stepped forward. He walked out to the front of the crowd and turning his back on the raised muskets of the marines he spoke to the townspeople.

"Go back to your hames and workshops. This is nothing to do with us. It's atween these men and Governor Scott and I think he is not inclined to argue. He and his men are likely halfway tae Brechin by now."

There was some muttering at this but the threat of the muskets and Robertson's words had the required effect and the crowd slowly began to disperse. The last to go was Betty Auchterlony. She stood and glared at Robertson.

THE BATTLE OF SOUTH ESK

"Ah weel kent *ye* for a damned Whig, Andra Robertson, and ah'll no forget this day. When General Ogilvy comes back we'll mak sure you get your answer."

Robertson was not in the least put out by this and answered in like manner. "I tell you this, Betty Auchterlony, the next time you see Ogilvy it will be when General Wade hings him and his Papist Prince fae the town cross."

"Ha, we'll see aboot that," she muttered and stomped off.

Robertson now turned to greet the Naval Officer. "Guid day to you, Sir. Andra Robertson is my name and I welcome you to Montrose although," he added, "ye've been a while in gettin here."

"I had not expected such a hostile reception."

"I fear there are many rebel supporters in the town, Sir, but some loyal men are still left, and now that the Navy is here we will soon put things to rights."

The young man looked slightly uncomfortable. "Unfortunately we will not be staying long, Mr Robertson. We are here for a particular reason."

"What do you mean, Sir?"

"Our orders are plain. We are to ensure that none of the ships in Montrose harbour can be used by the rebels or their French allies."

"And how do you intend to do that, Sir, if you are not staying?" asked Robertson in a low voice.

"We will remove the sails and rigging from all the boats in the harbour," said the Officer.

"You cannot do that, man! These men depend on the boats for their living," protested Andrew.

"I regret the need as much as you, Sir, but our orders are simple. We remove the rigging and if there is any resistance we burn the boats to the water line or sink them where they lie."

Robertson argued with the man for several minutes but could make no impression and eventually he and Cargill made their way back to his chandlery where he poured them both a large measure of brandy. "I made a richt fool o' myself there, Jamie," he said after a thoughtful sip at the drink.

"Aye, I fear there will be few loyal men left in Montrose if the Navy disables a' the boats," agreed James.

"Ach it's a bad business, Jamie, when our ain side dae us mair herm than the rebels."

For the rest of that day and the next the crew of the *Hazard* moved from boat to boat removing the rigging and sails. However, Governor Scott and his men had not been idle and on the evening of the second day they made contact with a French privateer who was due to land supplies for the Jacobite army. One of Scott's men was the harbour pilot, William Blyth, and it was under his guidance that the French ship sailed into the basin under cover of darkness. At first light she ran down upon the unprepared *Hazard* and under the threat of her heavier armament the sloop was forced to surrender.

Andrew Robertson stood outside his shop and watched grim faced as the crew of the *Hazard* were brought ashore under escort and lodged in the town tollbooth. Betty Aucherlony and her friends had come down to jeer at the seamen as they were marched away.

Now she turned to Andrew. "Weel Maister Robertson, yer Royal Navy didna last long, and German Geordie will be next to go."

Robertson stared at her coldly and replied grimly. "It's a damned bad day, Mistress, when honest British seamen are betrayed by their ain folk tae a nest o' French Pirates."

The Jacobites made great play of the capture of the *Hazard,* and even Andrew Robertson had to concede that it was something of a triumph.

"Aye Jamie it was cleverly done I will grant you," he said to Cargill a few days later as they sat together over a steaming pot of coffee in the parlour above the Chandler's shop. James was about to reply when their talk was interrupted by the distant sound of gunfire. Andrew Robertson rose and went to the window which looked out on to the harbour entrance and the North Sea beyond. He picked up a telescope which lay on a small table and studied the sea.

"Ah ha, Jamie my boy, we have a sea battle on our doorstep. Come and look."

James Cargill rose and walked to the window. Two ships could be seen about a mile from shore and the puffs of smoke and sound of gunfire indicated that they were engaged in combat.

"The smaller one in front is a Frenchie and she is making for the harbour," said Andrew. "The one behind is a British man o'war, a big one by the look of her, at least a forty gunner. Come, Jamie, we must see this at close hand," he said slamming shut the telescope and making for the door.

THE BATTLE OF SOUTH ESK

A great crowd of townspeople had already gathered by the time they reached the harbour. Several of the seamen in the group had telescopes and called out information about what was happening.

"The one in the lead is a Frenchie and she is being chased by one of ours!" called out one old fellow.

This statement struck James as rather odd in the circumstances. There seemed to be some ambiguity about which side the townspeople were on.

The matter was further complicated a few minutes later when another of the seamen announced, "The Navy ship is *HMS Milford*. I can see her name plain on her bows."

"Aye," agreed the other. "It's the *Milford* all right. She's a forty-gunner."

There was a slight bustle behind and someone pushed her way forward. James Cargill turned to see Mrs Armitage making her way to the front of the crowd. She came and stood beside him.

"Ah, Mr Cargill," she said, "did I hear someone say that the Navy ship was the *Milford*?"

Mrs Armitage was a widow whom he knew slightly. Her husband, a retired naval officer, had been a good customer before he died.

"Yes," he replied. "Apparently that's so."

"Oh," she said breathlessly, "my son Peter is midshipman aboard the *Milford*."

Several people overheard this remark and the word spread quickly that a boy from the town was aboard the British ship. One of the seamen turned to her and offered her the use of his glass.

She shook her head. "Do you think the French ship has done her much harm?" she asked.

"Ach not at all, Mistress," said the man. "Yon Frenchie is too busy trying to get away. Your boy will be safe enough I think."

The ships were now close inshore and the French vessel was nosing into the mouth of the river which gave entrance to the harbour. The ships were still exchanging gunfire but seemed to be doing little harm to each other.

"Why does the *Milford* not give the Frenchie a broadside?" asked someone.

"The channel is too narrow to allow that," said another.

It was strange how the crowd's attitude had changed with the knowledge that young Peter Armitage was aboard the Navy ship. It seemed they were now siding with the King's ship.

As the ships entered the channel they could be seen clearly from where the crowd were standing. The sound of the gunfire was loud, and in between, orders in French and English could be heard. The East wind had slackened but the grey sulphurous smoke of gunpowder drifted into the crowd causing some to cough and cover their mouths and noses.

"If the Frenchie don't change course soon he'll run aground," said one of the seamen. There was a murmur of agreement from some of the others, but no-one made any move to warn the Frenchman of his danger. They continued to watch and a few minutes later the French ship came to a sudden halt as she ran aground on one of the sandbanks in the channel. There was a muffled cheer from the men on the *Milford*.

"Well yon Frenchie's finished now, Mistress Armitage," said the old seaman with a smile of satisfaction.

The *Milford* now shortened sail and anchored about fifty yards to the stern of the French ship where she continued to fire into her. There was considerable confusion on board but there was little they could do to refloat their ship in the circumstances, and after a little they lowered boats on the side away from the *Milford* and abandoned her to her fate. Soon after, the *Milford* ceased firing and red-coated marines could be seen on the deck of the French vessel.

"Will they try to pull her off?" James asked the seaman beside him.

"No, she is stuck fast now until the tide turns and I think she may break her back when the tide is fully out."

The next morning, just as the man had predicted, the French ship was still on the sandbank, her back broken and her hold full of water. There she was to lie for many months until she finally broke up.

"Well it seems the French are not having it all their own way after all," said Andrew Robertson as he and James walked slowly home after the incident. Andrew was obviously pleased by the turn of events but James Cargill, mindful of his son's position, felt a chill of apprehension at the final outcome of this affair.

THE WHITE SNAKE OF THE REEKIE LINN

Louise Ramsay

Neish sat in the cave at the edge of the pool at the bottom of the cliff. The waterfall thundered loudly and a fine mist hung in the air. He had arrived here after a long and arduous journey – had made his way, scrambling and falling down the almost vertical bank that took him to the side of the river, and then got himself into the cave by negotiating his way across the stony floor of the waist high pool.

He was muddy, bruised, damp and tired. Wrapping his cloak around him he considered his situation. On the one hand he felt pleased to have completed his outward journey without disaster. He had come close enough at times but he was still in one piece. On the other, he felt worried about what was going to happen next. He had been sent here by his Master in Bologna, a great wizard under whom he was studying medicine, alchemy and the magical arts.

"Go," the wizard had said. "Capture the white snake that lives in the cave behind the Reekie Linn."

"How?" Neish had asked.

The wizard had been his enigmatic self. "The snake will be no thicker than a finger, no longer than an arm. You must catch it by the light of the full moon."

"How will I find the Reekie Linn?"

He looked at Neish scornfully "You will know it when you see it. The River Isla falls over a great cliff and thunders into a pool with such force that the air is filled with mist that looks like smoke. Why else do you think it is called the Reekie Linn?"

At the edge of the cave, there was a heap of sticks thrown there by the river in spate. Neish considered lighting a fire as the sun set and the full moon rose but decided it would alarm the snake, if there was a snake. That was the question that now plagued him. Until now he had been concentrating on finding the waterfall and getting to the cave. Now he began to feel stupid as he asked himself how likely it was that the snake existed. "What kind of snake is white? An albino adder? Is there such a thing? Is it likely that an adder would choose a cave by moonlight?"

Had the wizard chosen him for this quest because he trusted him? Or perhaps he thought that Neish, a Scot whose father was a great Norman Lord and his mother from a Gaelic dynasty, would have a good chance of finding his way about up here. The wizard would have seen his chance to get the snake that he wanted so badly. And never mind that his student was risking his life and missing months of study. Or was it because he wanted him out of the way? Perhaps it was a false quest and he had been fooled.

The long trap – a little longer than his arm, was set and baited with rabbit. Neish craned his neck to look up at the sheer face of the cliff opposite. He could see the dark silhouettes of trees high above him, growing on the flat tops of the cliff's buttresses. The waterfall crashed loudly into the pool and the bats hunted over the water. From time to time a tawny owl hooted and still Neish watched and worried, but no snake appeared.

As the sun rose the next day Neish's disappointment began to dissipate. He lit a fire then swam in the pool. Watching dippers walk nonchalantly into the river it seemed suddenly that anything was possible. Tonight was the true night of the full moon – the middle night of the three. Surely tonight he would catch the snake.

The hours passed and Neish's spirits sank again with the light. He wondered what he would do if there was no snake. What would become of him? If he returned to Bologna without the snake would the wizard not kill him? The day broke and he still had no snake.

All the next day Neish felt gloomy. The moon must be beginning to wane, even if only imperceptibly. He tried to raise his spirits by swimming and lighting a fire. Then he snared a fresh rabbit for the trap, caught a trout in the pool and cooked it on the embers of the fire. What did the wizard know, and why did he want it so much? What magic made this snake so desirable? Perhaps he had learnt of it from Michael Scott, Neish's countryman, the famous Wizard of the North.

THE WHITE SNAKE OF THE REEKIE LINN

Neish re-set the trap. There was a slot in the grass near the edge of the water and he placed it on this tiny path. He settled down in the cave for the third night. The bats and owls came and went. A breeze rustled the leaves but the air was pleasantly warm. Neish's tired eyes darted to and fro, looking for any sign of movement in the water or on the bank. Hours passed. At last the wind dropped and everything was quiet apart from the crashing of the waterfall. The fractured white disc of the moon lay at the bottom of the clear pool and then slowly a white line started to flow out of the water. The line, no thicker than his finger and no longer than his arm, flowed silently up the track in the grass towards the trap, lifted its head and flicked its forked tongue in and out of its long dry mouth, and then flowed inside. The trap sprang shut.

By the light of the full moon Neish considered the snake's enigmatic face with its strange sideways eyelids and its gleaming white scales. It had coiled itself comfortably, and seemed to be contentedly digesting a piece of rabbit. He converted the trap into a travelling basket, and resolved to take the snake back to Bologna alive.

As soon as sun began to tint the sky in the east he set off, scrambling up the bank, clutching at tree roots and branches, pulling himself up by his arms. He bounded along the path at the edge of the gorge and found his way out of the wood beside the bridge. There he met his guide, who arrived as arranged with his horse. He thanked him, tipped him generously then mounted his horse. The guide had suggested he might take him back again, by a quicker way than the way they had come, but Neish wanted to travel alone, relishing his achievement, cherishing his prize. He wanted to travel fast – faster than an old man's walking pace. He wanted to canter or even to gallop across those undulating fields. The horse was fresh and he was full of energy too.

He passed the farms he had seen on the way. He rode round the wetland surrounding the Incheoch, the island farm whose small boats were tied to the little wooden jetty, and Shealwalls where they were making hay, scything fields full of poppies, buttercups, and scabious. He galloped past Ardormie, perched on the edge of the hill, and as the sun rose in the sky he came once again to Bamff.

He had wanted to take another look at this place. Willows were reflected in the gleaming pools on the flat land and a dozen mallard took to the sky.

He admired the well-stocked south facing fields sheltered to the north by the heathery hill with its clumps of pine. In the woods the slender white trunks of birch reflected the sun that filtered through the canopy. From the spring at the Burnie's Head a sparkling stream cascaded through the ash grove. There would be no red deer as the King would be sure to keep them herded into the Forest of Alyth for his own sport, but here, beyond the pale, there would be good hunting too: wildfowl, roe deer, wild boar, beaver, wolves perhaps.

"Bamff," he thought, "the Pigling." His mother had taught him this old nickname for Ireland. His ancestors, the early Gaels must have loved this place like home.

He found his way to the Mill at Fyal and back down the den to Alyth itself. Oak and ash leaves closed out the sun and he rode along the pleasant cool path where the burn had cut a narrow gorge through the soft rock. He liked this country crossed by dens, gorges, river cliffs and waterfalls. It was different from his parents' home at Glenrothes in Fife – though that too was a fine glen, scattered with woods and well stocked fields.

Back in Bologna, the wizard narrowed his eyes. How many days' journey from Leith had Neish travelled? What was the nearest place to the waterfall? How had he made his way down to the cave? Wasn't it enough that the white snake was there for him to see? Naturally, Neish had become fond of the snake as he fed it titbits on the journey. It was harmless and seemed grateful for the care he took of it so he was horrified when the wizard instructed him to kill it and boil it up.

"What for?" he asked.

"How dare you ask me! Do you want to get your degree? Or do you want to be thrown out of this place with nothing to show for your years of study?" The wizard's eyes flashed red.

"You know the answer sir," Neish said quietly.

"Then do as you are told. Kill the snake and simmer it for three hours in three pints of water. Don't let it boil over! Do you hear me?"

"Yes sir."

"After three hours take the cauldron off the heat and come and get me. Don't touch the mixture. I will deal with the matter after that and you will leave and return to your studies. Is that quite clear?"

THE WHITE SNAKE OF THE REEKIE LINN

"Yes, master. Quite clear." The wizard was reputed to have the power of shape-changing. A student who annoyed him once was said to have been changed into a dog.

He left the room. Neish lit the fire and placed the cauldron on it, brought the water to the boil, and lifted the snake from its cage. He could not look into its unblinking eyes as he plunged the poor creature straight into the boiling water.

The journey had been long and difficult and Neish and was tired through. His fear of the wizard kept him awake while the pot simmered for the first hour, and his anger with him for the second, but as the warm steam filled room and the atmosphere grew soporific he could feel his body begin to relax into sleep.

"Ssssssssssssss" he heard in his dreams. "My snake!" he thought, waking quickly. But the snake was dead. The hissing was the sound of the mixture boiling over and falling on the fire. Remembering the wizard's words Neish leapt to his feet and grabbed the cauldron, getting some of the boiling mixture on his finger. Putting the cauldron on the floor, without thinking, he sucked his scalded finger. At that moment a curious apparition crossed the room. A moment later he realised that this was the wizard's cat, but its fur and skin had become transparent. He could see its inner organs: blood flowing around its body and food moving down the intestine. For a few moments he watched, mesmerised, but then remembered the wizard's terrifying instructions. He had accidentally defied him already.

Neish knew in the next moment that he must have some of this mixture. He saw at once why the wizard wanted it so badly, but it seemed to Neish that the snake had decided to give its powers to him. He took a small bottle and a funnel down from the shelf, and, this time using a thick glove, poured some of the contents of the cauldron into the bottle, corked it up and hid it well in an inner pocket of his cloak. He left enough of the mixture so that the wizard would not suspect that any had gone, and then went to fetch him telling him that he had completed the task.

Some months later he graduated with honours and left Bologna. The journey was difficult with a rough sea crossing. Disembarking at Leith he leapt ashore, overjoyed to have arrived safely. The men working on the dock were grumbling to each other. He set off into town, found a tavern and cheerfully ordered a pint of ale.

"What have you got to be so happy about?" the innkeeper snapped.

"Why is everyone so miserable?" Neish asked.

"Ach, have ye no heard? It's the king. He's sick and like tae dee. Best king we've had in years. If he gaes they English bastards'll gie us nae peace."

"Where is the king just now?"

"Dunfermline Palace. He's aye there at this time of year. "

"Thank you," Neish said, finishing his drink and going out into the street. He hired a horse from the stables and rode off towards Queensferry as fast as he could, getting there just in time to catch the last ferry over to Fife.

The guards on the palace gate looked at him suspiciously. "I am Neish de Ramsay, recently returned from Bologna and qualified in medicine. I have come to cure the King," he announced.

"No-one else has managed to do anything for His Majesty. We might as well let this young man try. Though I doubt there is much to gain, there is little to lose."

Neish entered the chamber. The king lay groaning on his bed.

"He has not eaten for many days," said the doctor at his bedside. "I doubt we can wish for more than a swift and peaceful end."

Turning his back for a moment, Neish took a sip of the snake mixture. He looked carefully up and down the body of the king. The bedclothes and the king's skin had become as transparent as glass. Neish identified the organs and looked for the source of the problem. He looked closely at his stomach. It was distended but the intestine below it was empty and nothing was moving through. The exit from the stomach was blocked by something dark and tangled.

"There is a blockage in the stomach," he said. 'If you will allow me to operate I think I may be able to remove it.'

The doctor protested at once "No, far too dangerous."

The king himself, though weak, was still conscious. Between groans he muttered: "Let him try. My life is worth nothing like this."

Pushing aside thoughts about what would happen to him if the king died under his knife he opened his bag and laid out the items he would need. The young doctor administered opium to his patient, and applied a herbal antiseptic to his knife and the area of skin that he was to cut into. He called for assistants

THE WHITE SNAKE OF THE REEKIE LINN

to hold the king down when the time came.

The king shouted in pain at the incision, but demanded that Neish carry on. He cut through the different layers, royal blood flowing freely, and came at last to the tough wall of the stomach. Pushing aside the festering contents, he found the source of the blockage. A great tangle of curly hair, the size of a fist, was jammed into the pyloric sphincter. The hair looked remarkably like that of the king's beard. Neish pulled out the hair-ball and set about sewing up the king. He wiped the needle and thread with antiseptic herbs, remembering what he had learnt from the Arab texts.

Wiping each layer carefully he stitched him up and finally, there was a neat straight scar with a line of stitches down his abdomen. The king's breathing was steady and calm. He had fallen into a deep opium-assisted sleep.

Neish waited at the king's bedside and watched him sleep, wondering if he would live or die. No-one in Scotland had, to his knowledge, ever successfully cut a patient open without a fatal outcome. In the night the king was restless and feverish. Neish administered infusions of willow bark to reduce his fever. By the next evening the patient was sleeping calmly so Neish left to rest himself, with instructions that they summon him if the king woke or showed any symptoms in the night. The next morning a maid came in and said: "His Majesty is much better. He has eaten a bowl of gruel and has sent for you."

He followed her to the king's bedchamber. The king was sitting up in bed .

"Are you the young doctor who cured me?"

"Yes Sire. I operated on you two days ago."

"I am very pleased with you and would like to reward you." Neish smiled hopefully. "I would like to give you some land. Do you want anywhere in particular?"

Neish's mind went back to his journey in pursuit of the white snake. He remembered the flat ground with pools full of mallard, the hills to the north and south facing slopes. "During my travels I admired your lands at Bamff by the Forest of Alyth, Sire."

"Did you now? I'll consider the matter."

Some time later Neish was summoned once again to the royal bedchamber. The King put his seal on a charter. Once the wax was dry it was rolled up and he ordered Neish to kneel.

"Neish de Ramsay, for saving my life, I, Alexander King of Scots give you the lands of Bamff, Fyal, Adormie and Kinkeadly, for your bairns, and your bairns' bairns, until the end of time." With that he handed him the charter.

And so on the 9th October in the year 1232 Neish de Ramsay came to own Bamff and the surrounding countryside. He built a tower on the rocky outcrop in the flat land at its heart. He was mainly known for having cured the king, but he spent much of the rest of his life using his skills and magic potion to help poor women at difficult births, and peasants with injuries from their dangerous work. At other times he enjoyed entertaining in his tower and hunting through his woods, fields and hills. He left bairns and bairns' bairns to enjoy his good fortune after him in the hope that they would still be there at the end of time.

DIGGING IN

Jean Langlands

There was a light covering of snow on Craigowl and the rich brown earth of the Angus fields had hardened with the frost. I followed my usual route along the old farm track which led across the fields from the Murroes to Kellas and Wellbank. In summer the walk was a pleasant one and the thick hedges of hawthorn and beech and brambles which lined the way would be alive with birds and insects. I had once seen a fox here in the early morning mist, a big dog fox wearing the finest of red fur coats. There was no sign of him today nor of any other life. An icy wind had stripped the last of the leaves from the trees and whipped them into confetti.

 I could see the grey walls of the farmhouse now and a wisp of smoke from the chimney. It had once been a thriving farm, where the men worked all the hours of daylight and beyond. Nowadays there was an air of dereliction about the place. The cattle and the poultry and the collie dogs were long gone. Even the garden, once loved, had grown wild. A feral cat lurked in the byre. I rattled the letter box but didn't wait for an answer.

 "Are ye there, Jessie? It's only me."

 "Oh aye, come in. I've got the kettle on."

 "It's freezing out there. Thank goodness for a heat."

 "Aye that wind's getting up. It's goin' tae be a cauld winter but nothin' we're no used to, right Mary?" She laughed in her usual cheery way as she got out the teacups and the biscuits.

 "What can I help you with today?"

 "Well, I thought we could sort out the boxes for the fruit. It's such a mess in the barn and if you could help me lift some tatties."

 "Aye, that's fine."

 She pushed aside some of the clutter on the table to make way for the teacups, then poured out the tea and we sat by the fire talking of times past.

It was something we often did now for neither of us was getting any younger. It was more pleasant to talk about the past than the future. It must have been ten years or more since Jessie's husband had died and they had no children. Still, she was determined to carry on with the farm. Said it was all she knew. Her parents and grandparents had lived and worked here and now she was the only one left of her family.

I gazed at her familiar face as she talked, the face of an old friend. When she smiled the lines of her face deepened and softened. There was a lifetime of experience on that face. I looked round the room. There were photographs and ornaments on the dresser, comfortable old armchairs and a rug on the floor, yet everywhere there were signs of dust and neglect. She had little time for housework.

"Have you heard from your nephew?" I asked.

"Aye, he's coming to pay me a visit. In fact he might come this afternoon."

"That'll be fine."

"Oh but he'll no help wi' the work. He's comin' for a nosey. I think he just wants me out of here."

"Has he said that?"

"Not in so many words. He pretends he's worried about me, says I shouldn't be living here on my own."

"Maybe he's right, Jessie."

"It's none of his business. I've managed fine here since Bill died and I'll no give up now."

"Aye well, ye've got plenty years left in ye."

"Well, you know me, stubborn tae the end. I've managed tae keep things going, what with renting out some fields tae the viners, then there's the raspberries and strawberries, and you and I have worked well together. Your Bob's been a great help as well wi the heavy work. I'll no leave here except in a box."

We both laughed and I got up to clear the dishes and take them to the sink. Jessie pulled on an extra cardigan and a pair of boots.

"Ye see this army coat, Mary? It belonged tae Bill; it's rare and warm and I found it in the cupboard under the stairs. It'll be fine for workin' in the barn."

"Oh, aye that's braw, well I've got my duffle coat."

The barn was cold and draughty and it took us an hour or more to move

DIGGING IN

all the boxes into the shed. There was a paraffin stove in there and we soon had it lit and began to stack the boxes and baskets into some kind of order.

"Mary look, dae ye see that cat across the yard there, yon stripey thing? Well it just appeared one day. I don't know where it's come from."

"Aye, I saw it as I came in."

"Well, it seems tae like the barn."

"Have you fed it?"

"It'll no take food and it'll no come near but it's aye watchin' me."

"Maybe it's lookin' out for ye."

She laughed. "Right enough, maybe it is. Dae ye mind the cat we had years ago, the black and white yin? It used tae follow Bill when he was in the garden. We ca'd it the gardener's loon."

"Aye, that was a braw cat and a braw garden."

"Look at it now. I don't have the time for gardenin'. It's all overgrown."

The morning wore on and we got through a power of work and all the while we talked. It seemed that Jessie's nephew was not a close relative. He was the only son of her husband's half-brother and he had been brought up in Ayrshire.

"He's no even a farmer. Works for some building company."

"So why is he taking an interest in you now?"

"I don't know but he's paid a few visits recently. Maybe he wants my money. Well, he'll be lucky because I don't have any."

The weather was worsening. We could hear the wind whistle round the corner of the outbuildings, like some demented creature intent on mischief. Then, as we made our way back to the farmhouse for some lunch, the dustbin lid was ripped off and an empty pail was tossed through the air. Jessie's army greatcoat flared out making her look for all the world like a ship in full sail. I gave her a gentle push in the right direction.

"Oh heck, let's get inside." she said.

Once in the kitchen, I noticed for the first time that she was looking all of her sixty-seven years, and that she was quite breathless.

"Are you okay?" I asked.

"I'll be fine in a minute, once I get my breath. It's that wind, it near cuts you in two."

I helped her off with her coat. "You sit down and I'll make us a bite to eat. The wind never drops here, does it, not even in summer?"

"No, it's like a person you can't get rid of, like me I suppose."

We had just finished eating when we heard the sound of a car outside. There was a screech of brakes and then the car door was slammed.

Jessie made a face. "He's no very canny is he?"

"Is that him? Maybe I should go."

She pulled back the curtain. "Aye that's him. That's Mike. No, you bide here."

Jessie's nephew was a handsome young man, of medium height with dark hair, yet he had a surly look about him. She introduced us and offered him a cup of tea.

"Have you travelled far today?" I asked.

"Aberdeen." He didn't look at me and seemed uncomfortable in my presence

"And you're going back to Ayrshire tonight?"

"No, I'm living in Dundee at the moment." He turned away and lit a cigarette.

Jessie gave me a look. "He's staying with his girlfriend."

"I'll go outside and lift some tatties for you," I said.

I left them to themselves and made my way to the field behind the farmhouse. It was still light and in the far distance was the sea and the lighthouse at Barry Buddon winking on and off, as if reassuring me that all would be well. The fields to the North climbed steeply towards Monikie and I could quite see why Jessie didn't want to leave this place. It was beautiful and it was all she had ever known. She was rooted here.

I began to dig out some potatoes and it was difficult work for the ground was hard. Just as well I'm younger than Jessie, I thought. Still a few years to go before retirement, though I couldn't imagine just doing nothing all day. Bob and I would get on each other's nerves. I gathered enough potatoes to last for a few days, then made my way back to the farmhouse.

As I approached the door I heard the sound of raised voices and so I paused for a moment and listened.

DIGGING IN

"Mike, I've told you already I'm no leaving here. This farm has always been my life and I couldn't live anywhere else."

"Farming is a man's life. Do you no think it's time you retired? This is no place for a woman to be living on her own, especially at your age."

"What do you mean, at my age? My mother lived to be ninety and she was hale and hearty right to the end."

"I'm only thinking of your own good."

"My own good? What's it got to do with you? Your mother was no relation of mine. We never saw any of you when times were hard during the war years and afterwards."

"I'm only trying to help you."

"Aye, that'll be right. You've got your eye on this place and I don't know why. You're no even a farmer."

"No, but my father was and you could at least consider my suggestion."

"The answer is no."

"You're a stubborn woman but I'll no give up."

"You just mind your manners."

I coughed and opened the door.

"Here's the tatties, there's plenty there for a few days." I looked from one to the other. Jessie had a grim determined look on her face and Mike looked sullen. He picked up his car keys and stormed out without a backward glance.

"For goodness sake, what's he been saying to you?"

"Och, I've had just about enough of that lad. I've tried to be civil to him."

She sat down by the fire and began to explain. It seemed that Mike had fallen out with his parents and was now living in Dundee with his girlfriend's family. It had obviously occurred to him that his Auntie's farm would be a good proposition if he could get his hands on it. He wanted to move in and take over the running of the place. But Jessie didn't trust him. It would only be a matter of time, she said, before he'd have her in an old folk's home.

"But it's your farm."

"I've never made a will. I suppose I'd better do it soon."

"Aye, right enough."

But the next day Jessie became ill and was taken to hospital. We were working in the shed when she got a bit breathless and wheezy and complained of chest pains, said it was nothing, she would be fine in a minute; but she was plainly unwell. The local doctor was out on calls and so an ambulance was sent for. I promised to lock up the house and to keep an eye on things for her. Fortunately, there was not much work to do at that time of year. As I looked back the old farmhouse seemed to have an air of gloom about it, the grey walls merging with the dull winter light. I wondered if she would ever get home.

I visited her as often as I could and Mike put in an occasional appearance although he didn't say much when I was there. She had accepted the situation with her usual good humour. The doctors said she'd had a serious chest infection but should make a good recovery, and sure enough about a fortnight later word came that she was getting home.

"I can't wait to get back to the farm," she said to me, "although they've been awfa guid tae me here. Mike'll be fair disappointed that I'm gettin' hame." She laughed. "He was probably hoping I was done for."

The plan was that Bob would collect her from the hospital but as luck would have it he came down with the 'flu. It seemed to be widespread that winter, and so it was agreed that Mike would collect her and bring her home.

On the day of her discharge I made my way to the farmhouse. I soon had the fire going and the kettle on and decided to make some scones. I switched on the radio and listened to the Scottish dance music. It would be great to have my friend back in her rightful place, just like old times.

Towards eleven o'clock I heard Mike's car come up the farm track at some speed. I pulled on my coat and went outside to greet them. The wind had increased in strength and was rattling the barn door as if trying to take possession of the place. I shivered, and then I caught sight of the little striped cat near to the byre. I hadn't seen him for ages and strangely he didn't run away this time but stared right back at me. Then the noise of the vehicle seemed to scare him for, without warning, he raced across the yard in front of the car. I could see Mike's annoyed face and then the car swerved and smacked into the barn wall. I rushed over to them.

Jessie was in the back seat and I managed to get the door open and helped her out.

"Are you all right, Jess?" I asked.

"Aye, I'm fine, just glad to be home. What an idiot ye are, Mike."

We waited for a response, but there was none. Nor would there ever be.

LOCATION – DUNDEE

THE SAVING O' MURDIE BOON

Beth Blackmore

Murdie stuck his wet, skeuch nose into the belly of the clean sheets when the wind in his backcourt shook them into life, like shrouds, all at sea. Only this time the hoor upstairs, as coorse a wuman as ye kin git, didn't come rushing to batter him. But his father did, for he'd carried the shame of his daft son's antics "roon meh neck fir lang enough", and he swore if he drove him roon the bend wan mair time he was for the Dundee asylum.

And behind the ill-grown father ran the big-boned Mammy, high-kilting her skirts with a face like fizz and inflamed with the passion to haul the father off the ill-gotten bairn. And after she'd done with the man, she drew the palm of her hand over Murdie's neb, pulled up his breeks, told him to fetch a stick and sent him to bang yon auld midden fir a wheen o mooses are flittin aboot the hooses. She still had a soft side for the demented craitur she'd half-skelpt the backside off for thirteen years.

And Murdie Boon banged and slobbered out his fantasies from morn til night amongst the muck lying about the battleground behind his house in Castle Lane where a score of bairns used him for sport; especially the lassies that dressed him up in hats and peenies and called him Big Jessie. He ladled muck at the bairns who chanted after him, "Murdie Boon's a girlie, he disna huv a willie." And after he proved them wrong, he breenged under the sheets throwing out the wash-tub spume and let it bathe his hot face.

When he was but a wee bairn most folks said it was a terrible pity to see thon puir cratur tied up for life with a mither and father like that, but they had little enough time for Murdie now that he had grown big and the bairns forever girning that he bent back their arms til they near broke. So the mammies warned them that Murdie's queer tinker-tongue and hurtings was the bogeyman in him trying to get out, and warned each other not to bother turning up at the Boons' door to complain about the temper-thrawin brute they'd spawned because they became rampageous and would clout anybody before they could draw breath. And so they kept themselves to themselves and told the bairns, "Murdie's aff his heid so gie him a wide berth."

And they did. On this very day, the bairns shuffled together to make a wall of nervous twitches against the bogeyman and remembered to shove the smallest ones to the front. They watched Murdie hang his arms and legs around the washing-line pole, staring and wondering at the sky, and waited for him to snap. Which he did, setting up the worst hully-bulloo ever witnessed by the mammies clattering down the plettie stairs with no more thought other than to save the bairns that had set out tae mak mincemeat o Murdie Boon, now louping out the closie.

Murdie tumbled headfirst into the cartie that struggled past the entrance and gave Johnnie Scott a richt fleg. The scraggy, spindle-legged lad had been running the cartie like the clappers for near a minute and was noo wabblin at the knees.

"Pul' in yer legs," yelled Johnnie, as he cast one eye at the palaver of bairns shrieking at the closie entrance and the other at the auld bloke scraiching behind him: "Bring back meh bunnet, y'thievin bastert."

Johnnie's chest was now fit to burst as he battled to control the homemade cartie along the narrow wynd with Murdie Boon bouncing so far down inside it that his bare feet were being chafed along the ground. His antics reminded Johnnie of a Halloween guiser he once tried to sell, only worse, as the old mummer didn't geitter on about a sore bum and sore feet, and keep asking "Whaur am eh gaun?"

"Haud yer wheesht," gasped Johnnie, as he turned towards the Greenmarket. So trachled was he that he wondered why he'd gotten it into his skull that daft Murdie needed saving from a snot of bairns when a stack of wooden paling was to be collected. And now he was sae dumbfoonered aboot whit tae dae wi im that he took a sharp turn into Gibby's yard and dropped the handles of the cartie. But Murdie never held a wheesht, and everybody knows that a geitteral bairn can't stop the rant of foolish chatter that spews out from time to time, especially when every bone inside him is rattled raw.

The late sun blinked on Johnnie as he coaxed Murdie, a finger to his lips, to follow him behind the shed. Murdie copied him, cheeky-like. They stood still as Johnnie listened for any rowdy, while Murdie made the pretence of giggling, which jammed on his jowls when a big roan-coloured mare plodded towards them, her nostrils steaming and her tail flicking flies that torment an auld nag that takes its time about everything. Murdie flapped his hands saft-like as she pee'd over some sticks.

"Dinna frighten Steamie, or she'll go rin-awa til she draps doon deid. She's no mine," whispered Johnnie. "Wait here til eh see if the coast's clear, then eh'll tak ye hame." Murdie's eyes lighted on the wet sticks.

"Meh mammy says yer sticks winna light a fag let alane a fire. An they gie her skelfs." He turned on Johnnie. "So she's no buyin ony mair." Johnny ignored him and keeked round the shed. Murdie pursed his lips.

"Eh'm no gaun hame tae git pit in the asylum. Eh'm stayin here wi him and eh want tae lie doon," he said, trying to catch Steamie's long tongue curling between his fingers.

"Steamie's a her, no a him," whispered Johnnie. "An yer staunin in her piddle, an eh only saved ye frae a lynchin, no tae huv ye as a pal, for eh'm leavin here the nicht and no comin back. So, eh'll be seein ye hame, richt," he added, hardening his voice.

Johnnie shouldered the door of the shed that Gibby let him bide in for now. "Oot o the goodness o meh hairt, Murdie, ye kin bed doon wi Steamie if she kin staun yer stink. But if ye dinna work hard, ye'r oot on yer ear."

Murdie squeezed in behind his new pal. "This place foofs better than meh hoose."

Strangely, Murdie calmed and lay down among the hay sacks and horse shite, bunnets and ravelling clothes covered with skelfs. And as if up to some devilry, slits of eyeballs darting from side to side and his thumb thrust down his throat, he hung two big fingers from his ear and growled himself to sleep.

Johnnie threw the bunnet on the pile and dug into his breeks. He took out his whittle knife and a half-crown and leaned his back on the wall. It was time to do a bit of thinking. He sensed the change in himself. Selling firewood for Gibby kept him from near starving to death, but although he had little money in his breeks, he had a lot of cheek in him these days. That morn, he'd pulled a big bunnet down over his face and swiped the half-crown Big Jim Macfarlane had laid on the shop counter to pay off some of his debt. Johnnie stared at the piece. It could cost him his life if the big red-headit man found out who he was. He turned from the wall. He would take Gibby's horse and cartie, maybe leave a shilling for it, and go to Glasgow. That was the place for a man to make his fortune.

But no matter how much he pushed and skelped, Murdie slept on. With a doleful "There's nothin else eh kin dae fir ye noo, Murdie Boon," Johnnie left the hut to harness the horse and fill the cartie with hay. When done, he sidled out of the yard and stood in the quiet lane. Nobody came about so he raced back for the horse and cartie, clambered up on Steamie's back and with hopes high, he jolted the reins and clattered out of Gibby's yard.

Steamie's hooves clicked over the last of the town's cobblestones and dug into the dirt road. As the gloaming settled down on the broom, an owlet hooted high on the arm of one of the ghostlike larches that lined the path to Perth until Johnnie felt lost from the real world, so close around him did the black night come in. He relaxed when the dawn swelled shooing away the mirk-night terrors in his head and he could see his hands on the reins.

The mare sucked on dry lips as Johnnie strained to unhitch the cartie. He stretched out his boot for the edge of the ditch and heard the water sloughing as, wi a thunderin drouth, Steamie slurped until the bottom of the channel was mud. Johnny leaned on the cartie. He did not feel the morning wax warmer on his face nor hear the far-cooing of the fat pigeons. He had other things on his mind. A man could sweat out his guts under fiery skies, fudderin aboot fir others, and have nothing much to show for it so when he got to Glasgow, Steamie was for the knacker's yard. Then he'd be a trades lad, make a proper pile of palings and save up his money until he could buy a year-auld horse and a fine cart.

Johnnie blinked out of his dwam as the haystack in the cartie shifted. Mice. He withdrew his knife and poked into the hay. Up shot Murdie Boon's big face, an ear-lobe bleeding so badly that the scarf of hay trapped under his chin caught the run of blood.

"How'd ye git in there? When eh wisna lookin, eh? Get oot," yelled Johnnie as Murdie sat up a-sniftering. With a face as white as a sickrife bairn, he slung his arms around Johnnie's neck and wept into his jacket. But, sudden-like, he slumped backwards with such a force that the bottom fell out of the cartie and him with it. The axle slipped and a wheel fell off, juddering like a spent penny, which panicked Steamie who took off down the brae as if doomed to calamity and didn't stop until she was well-winded.

"See whit ye've done," cried Johnnie, running after the nag, his mind addling about the broken cartie and the bluidie eejit that bewildered him so much that he would part company with him as soon as the time was right.

Paiching hard, Johnnie tethered Steamie and hauled the whimpering laddie to his feet. He pushed him to the ditch where they threw handfuls of water over grimy heads and faces, then he rubbed at the stains on their jackets.

"We need tae carry hay," he said, pulling up Murdie's shirt. And in less than a minute, his buttons were ready for bursting.

But it took a bit of shouldering to get the maudlin Murdie up on Steamie's sweated haunches and he slithered off twice before Johnnie could climb up at the front. Murdie's swollen shirt crackled as he tried to get his arms around Johnnie's middle. Clutching instead at his jacket, he laid an ashen cheek on his shoulder before closing troubled eyes. It took Johnnie three tugs on the makeshift reins and a decent kick before Steamie moved a muscle. Behind them the sun was scalding the sky.

Johnnie and Murdie laboured long hours at the first farm they came upon, its dour outby buildings sagging into the red clay. They worked hard for a decent supper, a roof over their heads and a bob or two forebye, until the day the farmer found Murdie keeking in the farmhouse window at his wife, a scowling snibbert of a woman if ever there was one; all angles and bones and big breasts which Murdie said she tied up with cloth, "so the bubbies dinna jiggle when she rins aboot cluckin ahin the hens."

And still Murdie kept growing; too big for his mind and breeches to cope and near high to the Perthshire farmer who agreed to take them on for a full month's work. Johnnie told the pig-man, "Wi toon hauns and straicht backs, baith o us bent tae tearing oot a wheen o weeding on than lang rigs for a haun'fu o pennies."

The farmer gave a low laugh as he watched Murdie stoop to fill his lungs before forking in a pile of rank dung, slow-like, yet was not there to watch him help unyoke the steaming horses as daylight waned. But the ill-luckit loon near-blinded himself as he stared at a plough being pulled into the sun; and when he plucked plums for the farmer's young lassie, quicker than a fox could take a hen, he was oblivious to the cruel glint of her blue eyes.

"Aye, an her father aye watchin us and ees heid swelling wi his Presbyterian ways," said Johnnie, warding off great pelting blasts of despair at his lack of progress. So Johnnie told Murdie what he'd do if he spied on the lass.

"Eh'll cut it aff an throw it tae the craws." And Murdie said his father had told him that as well.

The farmer hinted that he needed another fur-beast for the ploughing, so Johnnie sold him Steamie. Now slunken in the rump, Steamie met a miserable death hobbling up the dreel, and Johnnie had to give back the shilling. And Murdie couldn't be hauled off Steamie's neck until he was given her tongue, now slowly withering into a foul piece of black leather which kept sticking to the inside of his pocket.

"An aw the while," Johnnie said to the pig-hand, "onybody wi a grudge agin onybody, or a mind tae show aff, will tak it oot on Murdie. Eh've seen you trip im up, an Paddy O'Donnell hid im staun in the dung fir an hour tae grow clever. An somebody pit him in a barrel an rolled it doon the brae til he popped oot like a cork an near broke ees heid. Wish eh kent which bastert did it."

The pig-hand said he should teach Murdie to box and charge for it, and Johnnie said, "Murdie defint'ly hid the hauns an feet fir it." But the idea flew from his mind the next day when a big red-headit labourer walked into the Newton Farm, his jerking jaws warning that he might be seeking revenge for past affronteries.

Big Jim Macfarlane joined the hands on the farm without confessing that the polis were after him. He got a standing ovation and a few pennies for his rendering of 'Nearer my God to Thee' after supper and seemed unaware of the two sets of eyes peering in through the bothy window. More than one night cratur was startled as Johnnie and Murdie fell on their knees and crawled towards the high grasses, bellies rumbling.

"Eh've got this bad feelin, jist in here ..." said Johnnie, as he watched the dim lights burn deep within the cabin where the farm labourers were clustered around Big Jim who was hugging the whisky pig. The back of the farm was deserted so Johnnie signalled to Murdie to follow just as the gloaming changed its cloak for a black one and surprised an owlet.

"We're no feenished, Murdie. We're gonna pit stanes in aw the buckets.

THE SAVING O' MURDIE BOON

Then we'll lay low under thon hay." Johnnie's voice drifted. A little later, the owlet's head turned to watch them burrow under a stack.

Johnnie held his hand over Murdie's mouth as the bothy door flew open and Big Jim stepped out, skeerie-eyed labourers shuffling behind him, nightbugs dancing around their faces yellowed by the strip of light.

"Eh ken yer oot there, Johnnie Scott. Eh recognised ye, y'daft sod. By-the-bye, Murdie Boon's faither is lookin fir im." Big Jim waited. "His faither's offerin a reward: hauf whit ye stole frae me." He grinned at the men.

"If ye dinna gie me meh hauf-croon, wi recompense o a fu day's pay, Murdie's gonna get striped wi this rope." And he stung the ground with it. "Ye canna stay oot there aw night." The rope circled above his head. "C'mon, Murdie, eh'm gonna tak ye hame tae yer faither. Eh've got a lead, see?"

The men behind him spoke in near-whispers.

"Best ye baith come oot, Johnnie."

"Things kin git sorted oot wi daein some plain speakin."

"Ye should turn aroon an gang hame."

"Naw they canna! Eh want meh money wi recompense, then mibbe eh'll... That you, Johnnie?" A shadow walked in front of him.

"My lass says Murdie Boon kissed her when he gied her the plums," said the farmer's deep voice; his face killing any hope. "He needs a guid whipping." He nodded at Big Jim. "An I mean, a *guid* whipping."

Like the whoom in a lum, the wind veered showering a myriad of sparks over everything that fed on kindling. Soon a raging wall of fire spread across the haystacks and began to lay waste to everything. Nobody could douse it. The fire buckets were filled with chuckie-stanes and a big one was shoved up the spout of the tap beside the pig-pen.

Johnnie guided Murdie into the fell dark that lay over the clay-rig, gripping his hand as they stepped in the squelch of the bedded horses. They would keep walking until the cries of the bothie billies quietened and the grey light rose over the braes. Only then would he settle Murdie down to sleep under the budding broom. He had an awful lot on his mind.

MONKEY TRICKS

Ann Prescott

Hecate stood by the Bandusian Well and looked with loathing at rosy-fingered Dawn drawing crimson and gold streaks across the navy-blue sky. Late days didn't suit her. The water from the Bandusian Well permeated the whole of the Botanic Garden. It had a magic flux of 73.9 cigam but, for reasons Hecate could only speculate, some regions were more affected by it than others. Near the Well, of course, the force was particularly strong. As she watched, punctual to the second, the early morning mist coalesced into Titania's slender form. She ran lightly up towards Hecate, her pale gold hair capturing the sun's first ray:

"Hi, Hex. Ready to rock?"

"Don't start, Tits."

The sisters were to decide on an appropriate celebration for the Multicultural Winter Solstice Event, before the fauna attending the Preliminary Planning Meeting added their pitiful deliberations at noon. They completed their task in the Australasian Section, by which time Hecate was thoroughly bored.

The wind played on the elliptical leaves of the eucalypts; leaves that were bluer than the thin November sky. A koala bear was loudly humming along as he flew upside-down above their tallest branches.

"Bugger that bear," said Hecate.

"Really Hex," snapped Titania. "We've spent all morning fixing up a Multicultural Winter Solstice Event and you come out with a remark like that. What's the matter with Jim anyway? I thought he was most cooperative."

"It's the corks in his hat."

Titania settled her mantle of palest grey dandelion clocks more becomingly about her and peered up at the diminutive figure. The faintest of frowns fleeted across her ivory brow. As she turned back she glimpsed in her peripheral vision an unmistakeable streak of black fur.

MONKEY TRICKS

"Quick, Hex! Did you see that? It was that Howler Monkey again. Someone must have left open the glasshouse door."

"He'll be off to the *Araucaria araucana*. What gets me is why an animal with a brain like a flattened gnat's thinks it can solve the Monkey Puzzle. Honestly, Tits, if he's spilled any more beans under the Wishbone Arch I'll skin him alive. Mind you, that last time, you could have just let the woman's dearest wish wear off. I thought you were a tad free with the moon dust."

"On a scale of nought to ten I've heard dearest wishes that were more hopeless. She may not have been a scone off the day's baking but I'm sure they'll make a lovely couple. I reprimanded the Howler most severely afterwards."

By now they were in the Beech wood. The tree trunks rose like grey icicles from the deep pool of leaves surrounding them. The leaves glowed like burnished bronze. Almost, but not quite, they outshone the blazing amber eyes of Hecate's familiar, the great beast Mercaptan, who stalked at her side.

As this party waded through the wood there was none of the hail-fellow-well-met rustle, crackle and snap with which travellers were usually greeted, rather the leaves breathed a collective gust of relief, "It wasn't us," as Hecate and Titania stepped onto the path that led north to the Two Trees, where the faunae of the Garden were shortly to convene. In that birch grove no leaves thought it worth their while to linger on the greensward. Hecate noted with approval that the Minutes of the Preliminary Planning Meeting for the Multicultural Winter Solstice Event were fully occupied in reading their decisions of the morning and writing themselves accordingly. Before she could pass any comment however, she was half blinded by a flash of green light. Oberon entered from the west. He completed thirty two fouettés en tournent before addressing them:

> "My Lady fair, that most gracious Queen, Titania,
> Vile sister Hecate, thou Hag of foulest night,
> I grieve to bear thee such tidings of ill fortune
> that ..."

"Spit it out, Obe," said Hecate encouragingly.

He sniffed and silently extended his arm. On the palm of his hand was a frog who swelled like a small courgette, "uman to amphibian," it croaked. "uman to amphibian. Oots," it added with one eye on the glowering face of Titania's spearman, *Onorpordum Acanthum*, otherwise known as the Scotch Thistle.

Ann Prescott

"That bloody Howler! I knew it! He's taken his usual short cut through the Stone Roses and deliberately spilled those damned beans of his under the Wishbone Arch again!" exclaimed Hecate.

"I can't believe that any human's dearest wish would be to turn into an amphibian," objected Titania. "Of course the frog is such a very engaging creature," she added hastily seeing the courgette on Oberon's palm puff into an enraged marrow.

The Thistle intervened smoothly. "Your Most Gracious Majesties," he began, glaring at the inflated frog, "this amphibian was displaced during the incident. According to information received, the human in question is, or was, a boy child who, at his father's instigation, had assumed the role of a little green frog going under the Wishbone Arch hipperty hop."

"A boy child! A plump lad no doubt!" Hecate cackled expertly but her mind was racing. Titania got in first.

"If that's true then we have an extremely serious infringement on our hands. The child must be restored before Mummy discovers what's happened."

Mother Earth was currently in her menopausal phase and such a contravention of the rules would cause a storm that could wreck continents.

"That's well and good, Tits, but we've got to locate him first."

With one accord they approached the Two Trees and formed a solemn circle. Soft rainbows danced about Titania's robes and glanced off the seven trunks of the White Tree. Hecate's cloak of starlings' wings cloth dulled to sullen darkness. No light reflected from the Black Tree nor glinted from its hand-knotted orbs of witch's broom as she and Titania began the invocation:

"O fons Bandusiae, splendidior vitro,

dulci digne mero non sine floribus ..."

(O Bandusian spring, clearer than glass,

worthy of sweet wine and flowers too,)

The Well's dripping, seeping, response saturated the ambient air:

"Ecce; folia alta sunt sulcique gelidi in puteo

Bandusiae, in laco Macharis. et ipso in stagno foetido."

(Look; the leaves are deep and the furrows freezing at the well

Bandusian, at Loch Machar. and even at that stinking puddle.)

"Utterly bloody useless Utterance!" fumed Hecate, brushing off the rivulets of water that were cascading down her cloak.

MONKEY TRICKS

Wreathed in wisps of steam, Titania reached a decision. "This is going to take forever. Time had better stand still. Thistle, would you go to the herb garden and see to it?"

"Certainly, Queen Titania, at once" The Thistle bowed and withdrew.

Everyone else had a better opinion about where the quest should start. After much discussion, they decided against the Well and Loch Machar and adopted Hecate's original suggestion, setting off on the route that would lead them to the Stinking Pool. At the holly thicket a blackbird, who had failed to notice the lights flashing from the windows of the distant slate-roofed turrets of the castles on the Perth Road, found itself beak to nose with Hecate. It choked on a berry and with many a placatory cluck cluck shot to cover. Hecate smoothed her cloak and smiled.

Where the ways divided they turned their backs on the rough, heather-clad terrain of the North Moors and struck south-east into the Old Wood. At once their eyes were dazzled by the low winter sun radiating across the Tay. The trees stood grimly silent, shrouded in ivy. Their barred black shadows slashed across the copper-coloured earth. Titania was oddly uncommunicative. Hecate looked at her and observed that her toes were tightly clenched in a determined attempt to keep those ridiculous heels of hers from sticking in the mud. The ivy undercover on either side gave way abruptly to coarse reeds. They crossed the burn at the humped-back bridge and the undergrowth changed again, to the yellow and green leaves of wood geraniums that reminded Hecate of squashed frogs. The frog crouched on Oberon's palm took a more optimistic view, however, and bounced up and down croaking "ome, ome". The company exchanged significant glances.

They picked their way to the edge of the Stinking Pool and surveyed the mess of collapsed reeds and broken branches that served the Kelpie both as stable and dam.

"Maybe the Horse would help?" For once Hecate was hesitant.

"Well, I'm not rousing him," said Titania pettishly. "Not after the reception we got from him this morning."

"May all his dreams be nightmares," agreed Hecate cordially. "It'll be a Summons, then, Tits?"

The bottom road ran parallel to the river on the far side of the Pool. To the right all was deserted. To the left a visitor was occupied in measuring the circumference of Garnet Wilson's Sycamore. Hecate loathed that tree. She considered it vulgar. As Mahoud from up *Parrotia persica* was wont to remark on many an Arabian Night, "Mere size isn't everything", and everything certainly didn't have a circumference of 3.6 metres. She considered whether the visitor might be at risk but reckoned, on balance, that the yew hedge which shielded the Sycamore from the Pool should be enough of a barrier. By now the ever-attentive Thistle had returned and was in attendance at the wand tree. Hecate and Titania each chose a thin shoot, unadorned by delicate hazel catkins, and honed them on the granite boulder set there for that purpose.

"On a count of three…" said Titania.

Several things happened simultaneously:

Hecate's shadow loomed so tall that the trees shrank back.

Titania's robes glowed as yellow as dandelions in June.

The visitor found she was trying to write "3.6 metres" with a twig.

Two crows larking about overhead forgot to flap their wings and narrowly missed plummeting into the trees.

On a bright patch of grass, 29 frogs stretched and chorused, "Brekekekex, ko-ax, ko-ax."

"Bunch of hams," sneered Hecate.

With a graceful arabesque Oberon set down the frog he was carrying and spoke.

"O sweet Salientia, valiant Slug Slayers,
know that we have not roused you thus untimely
from your Winter dreams without good cause.
Tis said that one among you came not from tadpole…"

Absolute pandemonium broke out and drowned his voice. There were croaks of, "It's her over there" and "Don't kiss me" and "We're WYSIWYG" until Hecate thundered, "Quiet! I smell BOY."

Her long finger nail pointed to a bright green froglet about the size of a new pea.

The Thistle rasped, "All right the rest of you, dismiss!" Titania tossed some moon dust over the fading circle and murmured, "Hibernate in safety. Await the Spring with joy."

"Go easy with that stuff, Tits," cautioned Hecate. "Do you think we should

MONKEY TRICKS

risk a Summons again? Two in one morning are a bit of a gamble."

"As sure as the stars are her daisy chain Mummy would be on to it. We'll have to think this over very carefully, Hex."

Mercaptan took matters into his own paws. He picked up the minuscule creature in his enormous maw and shook his head vigorously. Hecate paled. Before she could act a toddler of about 19 months, wearing brown trousers and a jacket with a zip and a green tartan collar, had reached up, and was clapping Mercaptan on the nose, exclaiming gleefully, "at, at". Whilst the world held its breath Mercaptan purred "Miiiiilo".

"Well, all's well that ends well," Hecate remarked with a brave attempt at nonchalance. "The next job is to get this kid, Milo, restored to ..."

"His father, Majesty," interjected the Thistle.

"His father, of course, who is presently – ?"

"In the Stone Roses, Majesty. He is under the impression that he and the lad are playing a game of hide and seek."

The company took their only option and started on the trek west and north to the Roses. Their way wound through the Whitebeam wood where the silver leaves spilled over the ground like shoals of herring. Titania glanced at her sister and then whispered to Oberon. He kissed her hand and, executing a faultless grand jeté, disappeared into thin air.

Hecate kept strictly to the mossy path. She had a severe allergic reaction to anything of the genus *sorbus* and deliberately avoided looking towards the grove of rowan trees on her right. She moved forward with immense caution making sure that she didn't step on leaf or, worse, a cluster of orange berries that would bring on an anaphylactic shock. Titania, now with her shoes off, ignored her completely. She encouraged the child to toss armfuls of the glittering leaves into the air. Even Mercaptan joined in, lowering his great head and snatching them before they landed. It was all very noisy. At long last the blue and brown dappled shade of the Scots Pine forest ensconced them. There they strayed under the trees and trod the thick, resilient layer of pine-needles so that their punchy fragrance filled the air. Birds sang, albeit cautiously, and then only perched on the very highest branches. Milo made a small collection of cones and Mercaptan obligingly held them for him in his mouth. Hecate rolled her eyes.

Ann Prescott

By now Milo was getting tired so, when they reached the edge of the forest, Mercaptan picked him up by the back of the collar and carried him giggling and kicking across the grass to the Roses. The drystane dykes which curled and dipped to form their pastel petals were made from sheets of sandstone. Titania carefully set Milo on fresh bark against one of the concave curves of stones warmed by the sun, and passed her hands across his eyes. "You have had a lovely adventure. Now your Daddy is coming to take you safely home."

"More moon dust," groaned Hecate.

At Titania's suggestion Oberon was using as a vantage point the lofty, pencil thin, Cedar that soared like an exclamation mark above the flat lawns between the forest and the Roses. He told them that Milo's father had found him before the child's eyes had closed. He had picked up his son:

"Boo! Found you Milo!"

"at, at" said Milo.

"You want your hat? You wouldn't have it on, remember? We left it at home."

"AT!" screamed Milo until, exhausted, he fell soundly asleep against his father's shoulder.

As the last stroke of twelve died away, Titania began: "We are pleased to welcome you to this our Preliminary Planning Meeting of the first Multicultural Winter Solstice Event. I am sure you join with me in wanting to do all that is possible to ensure that the Event will be a huge success and a milestone in the Garden's history. Now I have apologies from…"

Hecate tickled Mercaptan's tummy and reviewed ways of skinning a monkey.

MR STANLEY, I PRESUME?

Ed Thompson

The West End Triangle . . . a small area in Dundee, defined by the Speedwell, the Campbeltown and the Tay Bridge Bar, where anomalous events sometimes happen.

I wasn't keen to go up Ford's Lane so late at night: it is dark and narrow. The cobbles can be slippery, and sometimes it smells like a public lavatory. Minus the essence of pine glade. But I couldn't wimp out of it after stopping to chat with the smokers outside the Speedwell. I had told them I was on my way to the Campbeltown. Going round by Pennycook Lane would have been preferable – it's broader and better lit, and even has a police station of sorts, though it's mostly closed at night. But Pennycook wasn't an option. Ford's Lane was the direct route, the one I had to take.

So I was half-expecting trouble and wholly unsurprised when it came. I had reached the darkest part of the lane, the bit where the trees behind the walls on either side reach over to form an arch, when a figure stepped out in front of me and said quietly: "Hey pal, know what this is?"

"No, I can't see."

"Sorry." He moved in the shadows, getting his hand into a patch of light. "Well?"

"A Stanley knife, is it? I've got one of them, with the retractable ..."

"What? On you?"

"No, at home somewhere."

"Aye, well I've got mine here and if you want to keep your skin in one piece you'll hand over your money pronto." His voice was confident, assured. Nevertheless I looked quickly round to see if we were alone. We were, or at least I couldn't see anyone else in the car park. There was a rustling from the recycling bins, and a suggestion of the scratching of sharp little claws. But that was it. If anyone was sitting in one of the parked cars, he was in the dark with his lights and radio off. I looked behind me to where the little group of smokers had been standing, but they all had gone back into the pub. Even Emphysema Pete, who could have whispered for help.

"Your mates are away, pal. You're on your own." He flipped the knife from one hand to the other, then back again. Very fast. "It's just you and me, and little Stanlee."

He seemed to bounce a little on the balls of his feet, enjoying the challenge. Time for diplomacy, I thought. "You're in luck," I said, "I've just been over to the Cashline."

"Luck doesn't come into it, pal. I was watching you. So hand it over and we won't have any grief."

"Fine, fine, no problem," I said, patting my way from one pocket to another, trying to remember where I had stashed the cash.

The trouble was that I had too many pockets: my trousers alone had four, plus a useless little fob pocket at the front. There were pockets on the sides of my anorak, and breast pockets, inside pockets, a pocket for a mobile phone, even a pocket on one of my sleeves. Then there was the gilet I had on underneath, which was stiff with the things, fastened with zippers, poppers, Velcro and including a poacher's pocket in the back. Handwarmers on the sides. Probably there were other pockets I had never found. Besides, two tenners (all I had taken out) don't make much of a bulge. Not easy to feel.

The Stanley waved. The blade was still retracted, but the menace was plain. And a definite touch of impatience: "Just get on with it, will you."

"I don't suppose you noticed where I put the money, did you? All these pockets – it's like trying to find things in an organiser."

"Yeah, I know. Look can you remember where you put your bank card? Maybe the money's in with that."

"No, I always put my bank card in the breast pocket of my shirt, so it doesn't get bent when I sit down. First place I tried. 's not there."

"Well have you tried that pocket on your sleeve?"

"I don't think it works. It's an accessory, a faux pocket feature. It's just a pretend zip – unless it's jammed."

"Jeesus Christ! I think I've been behind you at the supermarket checkout. Okay, c'mon over into the light. We'll be here all night at this rate. I'll give you a hand."

MR STANLEY, I PRESUME?

He took my elbow and steered me across the car park to where the sodium lamps from Hawkhill produced an evil greenish-yellow circle of light, courteously advising me to watch out for a scattering of dog dirt on the way. He turned me round so the light shone into my face. He was still in shadow, a stocky figure with big, busy hands patting me down like a bouncer, working at my pockets, opening and closing them.

"Here," he said, tugging at the strip of felt above one of my pockets, "does this open?"

"No. That's for Cocky-bondys and Humpies and Stimulators and such."

"You trying to be funny?"

"No. They're different kinds of dry fly. For trout fishing. Honest."

"Yeah? So which pocket do you keep your spare worms in, then?"

We were getting into each other's way, both trying to go through my pockets at the same time. He pushed my hands away. "Here, hold this," he said, passing the knife to me so he could deal with the zips of my fisherman's waistcoat.

"Right," I said. Then: "Any special way I should be holding it? I'm a bit new to this."

"Any way you like, pal, so long as it conveys a threat. Here, you seem to have an awful lot of paper handkerchiefs in your pockets."

"I know. I don't why it is, but I've never felt very comfortable about putting used tissues in litter bins. So they sort of accumulate in my pockets. By the way, why am I holding myself up? I mean, it doesn't seem quite right for me to be helping you to take my money."

"Well, I'm helping you to find your money. Fair's fair."

"Yes, still ..."

He paused: "Could be it's the Stockholm Syndrome. . . Or the sooner we find your money, the sooner we can both be on our way. . . Or maybe you're on my side because I'm a pensioner."

"What? You're a *pensioner*?"

"So? Have you got some kind of problem with pensioners?"

"Not at all, no. But I can see how some people might have a problem about being mugged by a pensioner."

"Ageist bastards!"

"Fair enough," I said. "Look, don't think me patronising, but is it fuel poverty? I mean, is this how you have to deal with your heating bills?"

"You mean *what's a nice girl like you doing in a place like this?* Well if you must know, it's got nothing to do with fuel poverty or the credit crunch. I just want money to buy stuff. I'm a shopaholic, see? I really need to buy things. Comfort buys. It's a compulsive condition, but nothing to be ashamed of."

"Oh quite, quite. We're all on a spectrum, I can see that. I know a guy who has to keep buying books to cheer himself up. He doesn't read them or anything, he just feels happier when he's bought them. They're a kind of fix he needs."

"Yeah, that's right. But your junkies, see, they can get methadone and suchlike on the NHS. What's unfair is that nobody's going to give me a prescription for a shopping voucher, are they? Or prescribe a subscription to a book club for your chum. All we'd get is counselling. So I decided to deal with it myself. Here, what's all this?"

He had found the bag of chocolates in one of my pockets. Cheap things, with mint-flavoured honeycomb centres, but good enough for my purposes.

"Choccies," I said. "They're not very good."

He helped himself. Ate two at one go, then tried another. "See what you mean. The outside is okay, but the filling is rubbish. You should get Maltesers."

"Maltesers are a lot more expensive."

"Believe me, they're worth the extra. Hey, what's this then?"

He had found the dosh. Under the bag of sweets, would you believe, crumpled up with the receipt from the bank.

"Right then, that's us sorted. T K Maxx first thing in the morning. Don't bother to follow me or report this. You'll only end up embarrassed having to tell people you were robbed by a pensioner. Oh, by the way..." he held out his hand, "Give us the knife, eh?"

"Wait a bit, I've been thinking about this. You've got the money, and I've got the knife. I was just thinking – only a suggestion, mind – but why should you have to wait for T K Maxx to open in the morning? You could start your retail therapy tonight by buying your knife off me. Care to make me an offer?"

I held the knife out to him. Perhaps he misinterpreted the gesture.

"Dear me, is that a threat? Well colour me scared. Try sliding the blade out on the Stanley, why don't you?"

I pressed down with my thumb, and eased the serrated catch all the way forward. Nothing happened. I slid the catch backwards and forwards. Still

MR STANLEY, I PRESUME?

nothing. "There's no blade in this, is there?"

"No," he said. "It's just a prop. I don't believe in physical violence. I find that violence of the tongue is just as effective, and it discourages people like you from going to the law."

A car came crawling up Pennycook, searching for a parking space beside the deserted school playground. I looked away to avoid the glare of the headlights. When I turned back, the mugger had disappeared. He was right of course. I wouldn't report him. I would feel a complete fool swearing out a complaint against an OAP who had used a knife handle to rob me.

I walked cautiously past the ranks of parked cars and out into the lights and traffic of Hawkhill. No, I wouldn't be reporting this. Besides, I was almost sorry for the thief. The sweets he had eaten were from my cleaner environment campaign. I stuff them with Imodium, and drop them along the routes followed by dog-walkers. It saves on green bags, which must be good for the environment, and the way I see it, a constipated dog is an improvement on the regular kind. Whether that goes for OAPs too, I wouldn't know.

RIGHT TIME, RIGHT PLACE

Nan Rice

Detective Sergeant Charlie Mahoney quickly scanned through the items in the *Police Gazette*. None were of particular interest, except the last: a 'Board and Lodging' fraud, where the guy was wanted by most forces in England. During the past year he had travelled the length and breadth of the country staying overnight at a good hotel, then leaving early and unnoticed the following morning, without payment. In each case the descriptions matched: he always used the Christian name Paul, but with a different surname, and there was a needle protruding about half an inch from the top of his left jacket lapel. Worth making a note of, Charlie thought, although such an experienced traveller was hardly likely to come to Dundee.

He sighed as he closed the file. This was not the usual Monday morning. The town had been particularly quiet over the weekend. He had been looking forward to a gritty, interesting murder. But nobody had even handed his wife a smack on the kisser.

He glanced at his three colleagues. The newly appointed, immaculately dressed Acting Detective Constable Stewart Grant was the only one gainfully employed. He was standing at the shelves reading an old case file and smiling broadly. Long-serving Detective Constable Ewan Watson was polishing the desk with the elbows of his blazer, whilst apparently occupied in solving the *Courier* crossword. The fourth member of the group, rakish Detective Constable Tom Hutcheon, nicknamed 'Smoothy' by his colleagues because of his glib tongue, had his hands clasped behind his head, left foot propped on top of his desk while the right was balanced on the spar underneath, thus allowing him to balance his chair on its two rear legs and stare blankly at the ceiling.

"Hutcheon!" Mahoney shouted. "Get your feet off the desk, you slothful bastard."

Startled, Hutcheon's foot jerked off the spar, his chair overbalanced, and he crashed sideways to the floor. "Oh, gee, Charlie. What a fright to give anyone." He jumped up, unharmed, and held onto the edge of the desk to recover.

"It's not a fright you need, pal. It's a kick on the bahookie." Mahoney was unsympathetic. He hated detective officers doing nothing, and he hated feet on desks. "You and Watson get yourselves out of here and get on with the job. Check the pawnbrokers, and when you're finished with that do a round of the scrap merchants. Find *some* offence being committed." When he was Detective Inspector these two would be back on the beat.

"Stewart, you come with me. We've places to go and people to see."

Once outside he handed Stewart Grant the car keys. "Left along Bell Street."

As they were passing the cemetery at the junction with Constitution Street, Mahoney said, "Would you believe they're talking about building a bloody high-rise parking lot on top of that cemetery? When I read that I skedaddled to the library to find out how long it's been there. The first body was planted in 1834, so the last can't be *that* long down. It's only 1974 for God's sake. Sacrilege, that's what it is."

He paused for a second, trying to imagine the change a parking lot would make to the area, then, "Right, Stewart, we're going to Mather's Hotel via Albert Square. Not a bad day, is it? We should've walked."

Seconds later, as Grant drove around Albert Square, Mahoney said enthusiastically, "See the Albert Galleries and Museum over there? Did you know that Queen Vicky had it built in the Gothic style and called it after her husband, that wee German fellow? Have you ever been in it?"

"Yes. My dad took me years ago when I was a kid. It was full of…" the flow of words stopped, then Stewart Grant said shakily, "pretty interesting stuff. And some lovely paintings."

The lad was learning in more ways than one, but Mahoney reckoned it would do no harm to extend his education further so, as they passed the Howff, he warmed to his theme. "Would you believe that was once the site of an old monastery? No? Well, in 1564 Mary Queen of Scots gifted this part of it, which just happened to be the orchard, to the people of Dundee. The Incorporated Trades people had their meetings there until 1776, and since 'Howff' means 'meeting place' the name stuck. It became a cemetery in 1828. Jeesy peeps! This has been some town in its day." He thumped his knee with a clenched fist. "I hope to God the City Fathers don't decide to make The Howff into a parking lot. The bogles would be after them. Now, let's head for Mather's, Dundee's one and only Temperance Hotel." A sideways glance showed him Grant's look of relief. "I wonder why it was built in that sort of triangular shape?"

On reaching the hotel they parked the car and climbed the wide staircase to the Reception Desk. A strong smell of lavender assailed their nostrils. It was somehow in keeping with the age of the hotel. The small, wiry, elderly receptionist looked as though she could have been there since the opening of the building.

As the detectives approached the desk she patted the bun on the back of her head, pushed her metal-framed spectacles further up her nose and said, "Good morning Sergeant. Lovely day, isn't it? Cold for October, though. Here's the book," and she turned the Guest Register towards him.

"Good morning, Jessie. Don't suppose you'll have many guests at this time of year?"

"No. Only seven. Three couples who come every year for a reunion. They're all ex-pupils of the Harris Academy. Then there's an Englishman who's here only for one night. He goes tomorrow morning."

"An Englishman? This him here? Paul Montmorency?"

"Yes."

"What's he like?"

"A lovely man. Well dressed. Arrived about ten-thirty this morning. I showed him to his room and he came down about half an hour later, said he'd be back for lunch, then went out. I don't know his reason for being here. Maybe he's working, since all he had was a brief case – although he didn't take it with him when he went out."

Charlie Mahoney was well aware that Jessie was nosey, which was good, because she was a fount of information.

"Anything interesting or unusual about him?"

"Only the needle sticking out from his lapel. I mentioned it in case he jagged himself. Would you like a coffee, Sergeant?"

"That would be great. In the lounge? And, Jessie, when you see the Englishman coming back give me a shout. I'd like a wee word with him."

"Has he been a bad boy then, Sergeant?" Jessie couldn't conceal her interest.

RIGHT TIME, RIGHT PLACE

"Well, someone has, but it might not be him."

Charlie selected an armchair from which he had a clear view of the lounge door. Once seated he whispered, "I picked something up from the Police Gazette this morning. Did you read it?"

"No Sergeant. I didn't have time. I was just reading my way through the informations when we left."

Mahoney related the story of the 'Board and Lodging' fraudster to his colleague, then glanced at his watch. "It's just gone twelve now, so he should be back for lunch any time. Thank you, lass." He smiled and nodded to the young, skinny, dyed-blonde waitress, who departed as noiselessly as she had arrived.

A few minutes later, and half way through their coffee, Mahoney heard Jessie calling him. He entered the hall to be confronted by a tall slim gentleman with an affable expression and a halo of silver hair.

"This is Mr Montmorency, Sergeant." Jessie stood where she was until a pointed look sent her on her way.

"Good morning, Mr Montmorency. I'm Detective Sergeant Charlie Mahoney of the City of Dundee Police. This is Detective Stewart Grant," and Charlie extended his hand. This guy wasn't the usual run of the mill crook. In his fifties, he was clean, tidy, well dressed in a grey-green tweed jacket, flannels, and brown brogue shoes. His complexion was clear and pinkish, indicating a non smoker. His handshake was firm. There was no sign of the needle.

"Good morning, Sergeant, I'm pleased to meet you. This is my first visit to Dundee. Haven't seen much of it so far, but it seems a very nice place."

"Thank you, sir. Come into the lounge and have a seat." Once all three were seated, he asked, "What brings you to our city?"

"Sergeant, it's hard to explain, really. I lost my dear wife a year ago." Mr. Montmorency lowered his head for a moment, then levelled his gaze on Mahoney. "I find life very difficult without her, and I'm reluctant to stay in the house. I rise in the morning and take the first train that arrives at the station. The local train takes me to Birmingham and from there I can get a train almost anywhere. Sometimes I have to take three trains before I arrive at an interesting town I haven't been to before. I stay one night and leave the following morning."

"My goodness, Mr Montmorency," Charlie forced a smile, "that must cost you a pretty penny?"

Mr Montmorency ignored the question, but said, "This is the first time I've been to Scotland, Sergeant, but I've been all over England. I know Dundee is a very old city, and thought it would be interesting to look around. I was a history teacher, y'see," and he again lowered his head.

Mahoney recognised the man had not been the least bit abashed by being confronted by the Police. In fact, he was quite relaxed. "You'll know why I wanted to speak to you, sir."

After a brief silence Mr Montmorency said, "Sergeant, I couldn't afford all these train fares, or to stay in hotels. During her last years I spent all our savings buying things to make my wife comfortable. After she died I couldn't get her pain and suffering out of my mind. So I decided to travel. At first I thought it was just a matter of time until the police traced me, and I didn't care. Then after a few months I just forgot about the police because it took my mind off Mary, at least for a little while. I'm sorry if I've caused upset to anyone." His smile became rueful.

"Well, I don't know about causing people upset, Mr Montmorency, but you've certainly wasted a lot of police time." Mahoney allowed a few seconds for that to sink in before asking, "What's your name, sir?"

"Paul Montmorency. I kept changing my name in England, but this is my first visit to Scotland, and nobody knows me here."

Mahoney couldn't understand the logic behind this statement. "Do you have any documents on your person to verify your name and address, Mr. Montmorency?"

"Oh, I'll have a look," and Mr Montmorency proceeded to search laboriously through his pockets. All he could produce was a five pound note from an inside jacket pocket and some small change from a trouser pocket. He placed the money on the table. "I'm sorry, Sergeant, that's all I have.

"Right, we'll go to your room and get your briefcase. Perhaps there'll be something to identify you in that."

"Oh, by all means, Sergeant."

Mahoney looked at the smiling face and made a swift decision. "It would be a great pity, this being your first time in Scotland, not to see any of our treasures. So, once we've collected your belongings the three of us will go to the Phoenix Pub in the Nethergate and have lunch. It's one of the oldest pubs

RIGHT TIME, RIGHT PLACE

in Dundee and the food is great. My treat. Thereafter I'll take you for a run around the town and show you some of the sights." He ignored the look of horror on Stewart Grant's face.

"Oh, Sergeant, that would be wonderful," and Mr Montmorency beamed as though all his birthdays had come at the same time.

As the three rose and started upstairs, Stewart Grant whispered to Mahoney, "Sergeant, do we have to go with him? He seems an honest fellow."

"We have to go by the book, Stewart. I know he hasn't offended in Scotland," as far as we know, he thought, "but remember we have to hand him over to the English police."

Mahoney beamed with pleasure. The sun was shining and he was having a great day. He extended his smile to include his colleague. He knew Grant would be disbelieving of the fact that the travels of the forenoon may be repeated, but well, he had a gut feeling it was all going to be worth while.

The two officers entered the bedroom with their captive. The young detective opened the briefcase and extracted a pair of pyjamas and a toilet bag. "These appear to be all there is, Sergeant. I'll carry this, sir," and he held onto the case as Mr Montmorency reached for it.

As they started descending the stairs to the street Mahoney said, "Stewart, you take Mr Montmorency to the car and I'll catch you up. I want a word with Jessie."

Jessie raised her eyes expectantly as the Detective Sergeant approached.

"Jessie, lock Room 104 and don't let anyone in until a fingerprint officer checks it out. I noticed he'd used the tumbler in the bathroom. We should get some fingerprints from it. Can I use your phone?" He lifted the handset, dialled, and once he received a reply, rattled off some detailed instructions.

As they entered The Phoenix, Paul Montmorency noticed the wording above the doorway. 'Here are your waters and your watering place. Drink and be whole again beyond confusion'. "My goodness, how extraordinary. And I see the pub has been here since 1856. Imagine a pub existing for a hundred and twenty two years. Amazing."

Lunch was most enjoyable, and Mr. Montmorency, being an extensive traveller, proved an interesting companion. After an hour's run around the city, Mahoney instructed his colleague to drive to Police Headquarters, where he telephoned the Fingerprint Department. "Did you get the dabs, Jamie?"

"Yesirree, and it's a Detective Inspector Hampton at New Scotland Yard who's compiling all the charges."

Detective Inspector Hampton was delighted to hear the Scottish voice. "A wonderful capture, Sergeant. He's really been an irritant down here."

"Well, I had just read the *Police Gazette*, then happened to be in the right place at the right time. The fellow wasn't a bit perturbed at being approached by the Police, which made me immediately suspicious, and his manner could only be described as," he hesitated, struggling for the right word, "overpleasant."

"What do you think his game is?" Detective Inspector Hampton sounded perplexed.

"I wondered that myself, so I played along with him. I took him for lunch, then a run around town to show him the sights. By the time we arrived at Police Headquarters I had wheedled out of him some of the towns he had visited in England and some of the surnames he had used, and I have a glass from the hotel bedroom with a good set of fingerprints." Charlie Mahoney paused for breath, than continued. "You ask what his game is? Firstly, he's a bloody good con man. Secondly, he's a jewellery thief. By the time I met him he had stolen a £3500 diamond ring from the best jewellers in Dundee. The needle in his lapel – well, it was simple. Before entering the shop he moved it down behind the lapel then, when the assistant turned away he quickly whipped the ring off the counter and hung it over the needle. If the assistant chanced to turn quickly, all she saw was him fingering his lapel. I kept my eyes on him the whole time to make sure he didn't dispose of anything, then I strip searched him as soon as we arrived at Police Headquarters before he had a chance to breathe. Needless to say, the first place I looked was the left lapel, and there it was, secured between the needle and the lapel. He immediately confessed. Of course I searched his clothing thoroughly, but there was nothing else. Still, a good morning's work, don't you think? I'm sure you'll find jewellery thefts in all the towns he visited during his travels."

"Great catch, Charlie. You'll be toasted in whisky the length and breadth of England for this capture. What do you intend doing with him?"

"I've already charged him and locked him down. Tomorrow morning he'll appear before the Sheriff Court and, since we've recovered the property stolen *here*, I'll request he be remanded in custody until you come and collect

RIGHT TIME, RIGHT PLACE

him. I'll have all the paperwork ready for you, including the fingerprint forms."

Later, when they were preparing the case for the Procurator Fiscal, Stewart asked, "What aroused your suspicions, Charlie? I thought he was a nice guy."

"Too nice, too forthcoming, all that apparently meaningless travelling, *and* nothing of a personal nature on him. Also, the needle was missing when he returned to the hotel. Why? Where had he been for an hour and a half in the morning? Stewart, never trust anybody. Not even your granny. And if you follow procedure right to the end you're bound to find at least *one* crime."

After allowing a few seconds for this lesson to sink in, he said, "Did you know there was something by McGonagall engraved into a slab in Riverside?"

"Excuse me, Charlie, got to go to the little boy's room."

A WALK IN THE PARK

Lesley Holmes

"Sometime before dark would be good," I yelled from the bottom of the stairs. I had to yell, on account of the persistent clackety-clack of the keyboard from the den.

"Can't we do it tomorrow?" Kate called. "Only, I need to get this report finished.'"

"Did I mention all the railings have been put back?"

The tapping keys paused. "Hmm ... What ... All painted and everything"

"Yeah, all painted and everything."

Things went quiet for a moment, then, "No ... no, I can't ... I've got to get this done." The tapping resumed.

"New gates too, apparently ... Well, so I've heard."

The tapping was replaced by the creak of the old floorboards as she crossed the landing and descended the stairs. She paused at the top of the first flight and ducked to peer through the net curtains.

"Hmm ... it *is* a nice day," she said. "Maybe some fresh air would do me good, and you could do with some exercise. Right, let me shut down the PC. I'll be down in a second."

Minutes later we were gloved and hatted, wrapped and shod in our Berghaus coats and walking boots – hers blue, mine green – ready to face the big chill.

At the corner of Wortley Place, a black cat was rubbing up and down against the north-west gate of the park – very creepy creatures, cats.

"Aw, *look!*" and before I could do anything Kate had crossed over to the furry feline. She took a glove off, stroked the cat's neck and tweaked its ears. Then for no reason, its paw lashed out and extended claws caught the back of her gloveless hand.

"Ow!" she yelled, snatching it back as if she'd been scalded. I shook my booted size nines at the moggy and it ran off.

"You all right?"

"I'm okay, the skin's not broken," she said replacing her gloves. "Thank goodness for your great big clod-hoppers. My hero!"

"Any time," I smiled.

"Ooh, look at these!" she said. "How long has it been since we had gates?" I smiled as she caressed the curlicues. I'd never quite got used to the wonderment she found in everything. She was always a 'glass half full' kind of girl, my Kate. Then she stuck her nose in the air and started sniffing. I didn't know why, but checked my boots just in case.

"Mmm ... smell that autumnal perfume," she enthused.

"Autumnal? You mean – wet dirt?"

"*No*. Well, *yes*, but, it's the earthiness. The earthiness of autumn. Take a deep breath and enjoy," she inhaled to demonstrate, "and look how golden and transparent the sycamore leaves are like – like amber jewels.'"

"Steady on, love. Don't get too carried away."

"Oh, you've got no soul Tom," she said giving me a gentle poke with her elbow.

"Nope, can't say I have," I said rolling my eyes.

"Och, you're hopeless!"

"C'mon," I said, "there's lots more to see."

I was anxious to get her far enough along the top path to see my pièce de resistance. But just then, out of the corner of my eye, I was distracted by a black flash that disappeared behind the private bowling club.

"What is it?" she asked.

"I thought I saw something. Hang on a sec ..."

"Where are you going?"

"I want to see what it is, that's all. I won't be long."

And off I went to investigate behind the clubhouse, but when I got there all I saw was glossy fur glinting in the autumn sunlight. Mr Moggy again. He looked back at me with hypnotic almond eyes. They shone like liquid gold and the black vertical pupils seemed to pulsate. Like I said, creepy. He hissed, exposing sharp white teeth. Then his tail stood straight up and spikey, like he'd been plugged into an electric socket.

"What is it?" Kate's voice made me jump.

"Oh, just that bad-tempered cat again. It *hissed* at me."

"Aw, poor thing."

"I'm okay."

"Not *you* – the cat, silly," she giggled. "So – curiosity satisfied then?"

"I suppose," then I took her hand, "C'mon, there's something I want to show you."

"As long it's not anymore of *that*," she said pointing to the graffiti on the ancient toilet block. The 'Ladies' and 'Gentlemen' labels above the doors had been all but obliterated by spray paint.

"Never mind that." I suppose I should've been more concerned but I had other things on my mind.

"It's not right, you know," she persisted.

"I know," I said, "but there's nothing we can do. And look, doesn't this make up for it?"

Here was the perfect spot. From here you could see ... well ... everything. From here she could see all the things she loved: the replanted rose gardens, the tree-lined curving pathways like flat black ribbon, the old weeping oak protected by a new willow fence, and most of the now leaf-littered southern parkland beyond. Only the back of the pavilion could be seen from here, but we'd get to that later. I let her drink it all in, crossed my fingers behind my back and waited.

"This is stunning!" she gasped. "And look ... there, there," gesticulating like an excited child at the newly built playgrounds. There were two – one with miniature swings and slides for toddlers, the other with rope bridges and climbing frames for the more adventurous. And that didn't include us - we were way past adventurous.

I pointed out the old weeping oak, "Can you believe *that's* still alive?"

"Oh, remember how we used to canoodle under its branches?" She snuggled close. "How old do you think it is?"

"Pretty old," I said. "There'll be a young sapling being nurtured somewhere to replace it, like they do with all old things."

"Oh, you old misery guts!" she chastised, then, "What's that building there? It looks a bit odd." She'd spotted the only blot on the landscape – the new Community Centre. Just then I saw a boy – no more than eleven or twelve by my reckoning – hunkered down by the building. He was dressed in black, a

A WALK IN THE PARK

back pack slumped on the ground beside him. I was curious; what was he up to?

"Can you see what that boy's doing?" I asked.

"What boy?"

"*There*," I turned back pointing, but he'd vanished.

"Are you sure it wasn't that cat again, Tom? Ooh," she said putting on a scary voice, "maybe it's Grissel Jaffray's cat."

"Who?"

"You know ... the old Dundee witch."

"What's a witch got to do with anything?"

"Oh, *Tom*, you must have heard the legend of Grissel Jaffray's cat."

"I don't know anything about any legend."

"You must do. Her cat haunts the park, to test the mettle of the people who come here."

"Oh rubbish!" I said shivering, "C'mon ... I'll race you to the pavilion."

"Race? Yeah ... right," she said.

I got there first and stood on the main promenade right in front of the building and waited for her.

"Oh," she said, "they've made a good job of that."

"It's Renaissance, you know," I said. "These are a 'loggia of Doric columns'. It's an architectural term."

It had all been in the literature I'd been sent and I was about to explain but she wasn't interested. She'd spotted that boy and we were close enough to hear the unmistakable scoosh of an aerosol.

"It's *him*, he must have done the other damage," I accused setting off toward him.

"Tom, what're you going to do?"

"I can't just stand by ... "

"But you don't know anything about him. He could be dangerous. He might be from one of those estates, you know, where the shops don't have windows. What if he has a knife? *Don't* Tom!"

"No, I'm not letting him deface the very building where we're going to renew our vows!" As soon as I'd said it, I wanted to bite my tongue off.

"What did you say?"

"Oh, hell – I didn't mean – I wanted it to be – oh, hell!"

"What's this all about, Tom?"

"Well, the thing is, it's a civil marriage venue now and, I thought, you know, with our anniversary coming up. I've booked it you see. I thought we could renew our vows here."

Her jaw dropped. Whether in stupefied shock or happy amazement, I couldn't tell. But she stood on tiptoe and kissed me – so I took that as a good sign – before she turned away to peer inside the new glass frontage. I crossed my fingers again, but I knew it would be okay.

I had an advantage, you see. I'd been inside already. It'd all been cleaned up: spotlights hung from ceiling gantries, there was a lectern – where the Registrar would stand – and rows of chairs for the guests. I could see it all: friends and family in their finery and Kate, my darling Kate, would be the best looking woman in the room. Even now, there were huge displays of lemon cadmium and snow-white blossom inside, and Sir David Baxter sheltered in his little niche. He'd come home at last – well, his statue had anyway.

I walked up behind her and wrapped her in my arms, "Well, what do you think?"

"What a perfect place," she sighed.

Then I heard it. Scoosh. Bugger! It was him again! I ran in the direction of the sound, around the side of the pavilion. There he was.

"Hey! Hey You!" I called. "What the hell do you think you're doing?"

The boy looked round.

"That's right, it's you I'm talking to!"

He stood as still as Sir David and looked right through me as if I didn't exist. He didn't look at all worried that I'd seen him.

"Mind yer ain business, ye auld fart," he said, then disappeared to the back of the pavilion. I followed but when I turned the corner there was no back pack, no aerosols and no boy. Just that irritating black cat, rubbing his face with a wet paw. "Damn!"

Footsteps crunched behind me. "Where is he?" asked Kate.

"I don't know. Disappeared. I can't see him anywhere."

"Oh, good," she sighed, "then we can forget about him."

"But ... "

"He's gone. Probably run a mile from the old geezer with the big feet."

"Do you think so?"

A WALK IN THE PARK

"Yes. C'mon, how do we get inside this place?"

"Oh, that's all sorted," I boasted, checking my watch. "Give it ten minutes – someone from the Registrar's office will be here to show us around. Will that do you?"

"Course it will," she smiled. "What about a wee reception afterwards? Nothing too expensive ... "

"Anything you want, love," I said, patting her hand.

The noise of children returning home from school made me realise that our ten minutes, and more, were up.

"I don't think anyone's coming," I said. "Let's go. My bum's getting frozen."

"Aw, but I *really* wanted to go inside."

"Don't worry. I'll phone tomorrow. You'll get your tour round the pavilion."

Scoosh. There it was again. I stiffened.

"Leave it," she said, grabbing my arm.

I shrugged her off and stood up. "No, you were right. It's not right ...." and strode toward the rear of the pavilion. The boy, who was cramming things into his bag, looked straight at me.

"C'mon then granddad! Catch me if ye can," he dared, then loped off toward the playgrounds.

I gave chase – I was faster than he realised, faster than I realised – and I managed to grab the hood of his parka almost strangling him as he lurched to a sudden halt.

"Tom, be careful!" shouted Kate.

"Lemme go!" yelled the boy.

"You're coming with me to the Ranger's Lodge."

"They'll no dae anythin' tae me, ehm jist a kid."

"A lot of work's been done here, don't you care?"

"'S no meh problem."

"Yes it is. Don't you realise how much you're spoiling the place for everyone?"

"Wha'ever!"

"You just don't give a damn, do you?"

"They can wash it aff. It'll gie them sumthin' ta dae."

All the while the boy struggled but I managed to hold him. Then, when we reached the weeping oak he twisted under my arm and gave me a mighty kick, hard on the shin. I grabbed my leg and fell backwards onto a nearby bench.

"Fuck aff, ye miserable auld death-dodger! It's only a park!" he shouted as he escaped back down the path.

I looked up just in time to see Kate stick out her foot, tripping the boy, who fell with a thud to the rough tarmac. I hobbled over to them and hauled him to his feet.

"Right, you little bugger! You're coming with me!"

I dragged him toward the Lodge, past the disapproving looks of a couple of bouncing joggers craning their necks trying to work out what was happening.

"Hey!" called the woman, "what's going on?"

I stopped and glanced back. "Don't you worry yourselves. I've got it all in hand."

"I'm sorry," she continued, "but there are laws against manhandling a child like that, even if they're your own."

"Oh, he's not one of mine. None of mine would dare –"

"I think you should take your hands off him," the man butted in.

"Yeah, y've hud it now. Y'd better lemme go."

I let out a sigh. "Look, I caught the lad red-handed. I'm taking him to the Ranger's Lodge."

The joggers turned toward each other; her mouth was flapping nineteen to the dozen in time with her waving arms. He seemed keen to move on. I decided not to hang around.

"No, wait!" shouted the woman. "We're coming with you."

"What for?" Now I was irritated.

"Witnesses," she said.

"Thanks all the same but I don't need any witnesses. My wife saw him too."

The joggers exchanged puzzled looks. "Not for you – for *him*," said the man. "We'll come with you, just to make sure there's fair play."

Fair play! The boy had practically broken my shin bone. It's a wonder I wasn't charging him with assault. "Oh, come on, Kate," I said shaking my head, "let's get this over with."

We all traipsed up to the Ranger's Lodge, Kate and I either side of the boy, with me keeping a tight grip on his hood to prevent further escape. The joggers, true to their word, followed a short distance behind.

The door of the Lodge opened just as we arrived, "Well, what've we got

A WALK IN THE PARK

here then?" asked the Ranger.

"Caught him red-handed," I said, "spray painting the back of the pavilion."

"Oh ye did, did ye?" he said, then looking down at the boy, "What've ye got to say fer yersel, laddie?"

Before the boy could open his mouth, the joggers had to get their tuppence worth in. "Look, excuse me,"'said the woman, "but this man, well, he's been manhandling the child all the way round the park."

"Now that's not true!" Kate jumped to my defence.

"All I'm saying is, we don't know who you are, do we?"

The Ranger eyed us one by one, then stepped to one side inviting us in. He directed us to a small office and we all squeezed in. Kate sat on the only chair, while the rest of us lined up against one blank wall, as if we were in an identity parade.

"Right, who's going to start?" asked the Ranger.

"Well, as I said, we caught him red-handed," I kicked off, giving my shin another wee rub. "I won't even press charges for the assault."

"Come on now," said the woman. "He's just a wee boy. Are you asking us to believe *he* assaulted *you*? I don't *think* so." She looked across at the Ranger. "He could be one of them – them child molesters for all we know."

"Oh, for goodness sake!" I snapped.

"That's a serious allegation, madam," interrupted the Ranger, "and not one I'm equipped to deal with. I'll have to call the police, I'm afraid," and he turned to the phone on the desk, but his broad back muffled any conversation.

Why couldn't I have left things alone like Kate said? We'd be home now, in front of the fire with a nice cup of tea. But no, I had to stick my nose in. Will I ever learn? She'd gone really quiet – not a good sign – so I hunched down beside her to give her what comfort I could.

"Don't worry, it'll be fine."

The joggers jabbered amongst themselves. I wished I could bang their heads together. A child molester? *Me* – a father of three? Then I looked across at the boy. He looked back at me with hypnotic almond eyes – they shone like gold and the pupils seemed to pulsate. Then he grinned, exposing sharp white teeth, and I could have sworn he hissed.

I turned to the Ranger but, "Right, they're on their way," he said looking at each of us in turn, taking inventory. "Where's the boy?"

"Right there," I pointed, but kept my eyes averted not wanting to look at him again.

"What are you talking about, man? Where is he?"

"*There*," but when I looked he'd gone. "Well he was there a moment ago."

"So, anyone see where the kid went?" asked the Ranger. "Can't do anything without him. We'll look like real prats when the police get here if he's not found. Right, everybody outside now, I want to know where that kid went!"

As I stood up something soft brushed against my leg and I looked down, straight into Mr Moggy's eyes – eyes that shone like liquid gold.

THE WINKLE SELLER

Jane O'Neill

He came in summer, the Winkle Seller.
His stall a beat-up Silver Cross,
boat-shaped, with swan-necked handles,
heaped with forage from the low tide.

Children from the Crescent and the Street,
skipped by his side, as though to music;
lured by the salt and the sea weed.
And the pram rocked on its straps, as he stopped to sell.

Paper cones shaped with a twirl and a twist,
he rattled the winkles in a crazed, chipped cup,
a bright pin nipped from his lapel,
exchanged for a tuppeny buy.

With an expert flick, the trapdoors flew
like black confetti to the ground;
boiled and salted, now a soft chew,
and the winkles peeped from their shells.

But, as the summer tailed to an end,
I lost my milk teeth, turned from seven to eight,
grew an inch and a half, and followed
the sign "To The Grassy Beach" – where

with a pickle jar, and a sister to take my hand,
I teetered on legs like spindles, slid on tangles of weed,
and snapped winkles from their glue: their coiled bodies
retreating beneath the horny plate.

Jane O'Neill

With frocks tucked into knickers we ran to meet
the tide; a clear green rush on our pink-cold feet.
A wader sat on guard: an eye watched, a beak dribbled,
as the jar lolled in a pool and filled with brine.

I held the jar up by the hairy string,
as moving coils of black and yellow and white
– a fleshy creeping on flat muscly feet –
rasped their way up the glass.

And I knew, if I didn't return them to their tide,
they would crawl past the string, and eat.

THE RINGO KID

John Mooney

I like cowboys. Last night I went to see The Ringo Kid with Davie and Geordie and Billy. Ringo had a gunfight with Johnny Waco. I shot Davie and Geordie and Billy three times on the way home. Ringo walked with his hands over his guns so he would be ready to shoot. He sometimes flicked his fingers and his spurs jangled. Ringo never ever shot someone in the back. I didn't shoot Davie or Geordie or Billy in the back. Me and Flame rode back from the pictures. We went through the Sierra Nevada then over the Oregon Pass and Mum was waiting at the end of the close. She wasn't crying like she was when she gave me the sixpence for the pictures. Betty my sister had to go to the doctors. She was crying when she came back. When mum was putting me to bed I asked if I could change my name. I like Ringo better than John. She told me I could and to go to sleep and she started crying again.

I stayed awake all night. Ringo McCallum, Ringo McCallum, Ringo McCallum. Hi Ringo, Hi Davie. Hey Ringo are you going to the pictures? Yup Geordie. I liked that.

Next day Mum took me to Aunty Betty's. Aunty Betty used to be Mum's sister when they were wee. We got cakes. When we got there Aunty Betty took me into her bedroom. She gave me ginger and a comic and told me to play. I think Mum and Aunty Betty had their cakes in the front room. We went home after we got the cakes.

I asked Mum if I could go round to Davie and Geordie and Billy to tell them that my name was Ringo. She said to be back before eight. Geordie lives in the next close. He's got two stairs and two landings. I can run doon my stairs faster than anybody. Faster than Bert who comes to see my brother Jimmy. He's a man. Sometimes he sees Betty as well.

Geordie's stair has a lavvy half-way up. I was needing but the door was locked. I just did it on the door and it started to run doon the steps. I knocked

John Mooney

on Geordie's door. He opened the door. I said I'm changing my name to Ringo. He said he wasn't coming out to play and closed the door. I went out on to the landing and keeked in through his window. It was dim cos the gas was at a low peep. Geordie and his mum were sitting beside the fire and his mum was crying. She had a hankie at her nose. She was crying cos she had the cold. There was a big candle on a big long box in the room cos it was dim and Geordie's gran was there. She must have had the cold as well and she had beads in her hands cos she went to church. I could run doon Geordie's stairs two steps at a time. Sometimes three at a time if I wanted. Geordie's gran was in black and so were her beads. I was going doon Geordie's stair and I heard a man coming up. I knew it was a man cos he said bugger three times when he got to the lavvy so I went back up and stood two steps up the other stair. He went into Geordie's house. He was in black with a black hat on.

Billy lived in Dummy Smiths and that was across the road where the buses pass. Billy had three stairs and three landings. You could see the railway bridge and the ferries from Billy's back room. The lamps were lit. I ran up the first two stairs fast. I stopped awhile before going up the last stair. It was really dark cos the light was out. A wifie's voice said, who's that, from up the stairs where the lavvy was and I said me. She said, oh come up then and I knew it was Irene. Irene lived next door to Billy. I went up the stairs with my sandshoes on. Tommy Bruce's big brother said you could creep up on an Indian if you had sandshoes on and he wouldn't ken. I crept up. I got up half way where the lavvy was on the stair. It was awfy dark and Irene whispered, wait, wait. So I did. After a while Irene said, oh Andy, oh Andy and she was pechin like Rover, Billy's Aunty Peg's dog. I said I'm John and Irene screamed and a man said bloody hell and I ran up the stairs. I think Irene and the man got a flegg.

I knocked on Billy's door. Billy's Mum opened the door and shouted for Billy. Billy's Mum said hello to me and asked how was I doing and she had big red lips on her face and she had big shoulders. She was smoking and she had a tumbler in her hand and their gas lamp was really bright and the wireless was really loud. She asked me how was Betty. Sometimes Billy's Mum didn't speak to me if she saw me in the street. She always spoke to me when she had the big red lips. Billy came to the door and I said Hi. Billy's mum said close the door for the draught so he did. I said my name is now Ringo. Billy said he had a new

THE RINGO KID

Captain Marvel comic from his aunty in America and did I want to see it? I said yes, and he went back into the room and left the door open. Billy's mum was standing at the main. She was cooking soup and tasting it. That's what was in the tumbler. I could see the steam from the big pot and smell the carrots and the turnip and the kale. Billy's dad was sitting next to the main coughing and singing to the wireless. He was tasting the soup as well. It was Bing Cropley singing. I know him cos my dad used to listen to him and whistle. Billy's dad started to cough again and I heard him spit. He must have spat in the fire cos there was a great big sizzle. Billy's dad was a good spitter. Billy's mum shut the door. I stood there for a long time then I went out onto the landing. Over the railings there was washing hanging on the ropes that were lassooed to the big poles at the back of the shelters. The light from Billy's window was shining. I saw a pair of Billy's mum's things. They were blowing in the wind and had pink bows. Inside Billy's house I could hear them speaking. Billy's dad said it was Bert's father. I didn't know Bert had a father. I don't know what it was that Bert's father did. After a while I left and went to Davie's. I didn't get to see Billy's new Captain Marvel comic. I think he just forgot about me.

Davie didn't have a stair. He had an entrance. That's what Mrs Rae, his mum, said, an entrance. The entrance was like our close and when you passed Davie's house, a stair went up to more houses above. The entrance had tiles half-way up the walls and if you stood on Billy's back you could see inside Davie's house from the pavement outside. Mum said they were posh. There was a car in Davie's street. A big black one with wheels.

Mrs Rae was polishing her door when I came in the entrance. I walked halfway in and stopped. She saw me and said David, David, are you there? She didn't stop polishing. She said it just like our teacher says it. She asked me how mum was and if Betty was still working. I never knew what to say when Mrs Rae asked me questions. Davie came out and asked his mum if he could play. Davie's mum said yes, but only for ten minutes then he had to do his violin. Davie had loads of marbles. He had them in a big jar with a golliwog on the lid. We walked to the end of the entrance. The bit away from Mrs Rae. I told him my name was now Ringo McCallum but I whispered it like it was a secret and he whispered back. He asked what my mum had said about it. But mum came to the end of the close and said it was bed-time. Mrs Rae asked her how

John Mooney

she was but mum said it was late and she had to hurry.

I looked out the window. It was Saturday morning. I knew it was Saturday cos everybody walked quicker on Saturdays and they whistled and smiled. Mum said I had to go to the sosh for the messages and she gave me a line and the coupons. I asked if I could wear my snake belt and she said yes. I liked going to the sosh. There were chairs there to sit on and the counter where you were served was two miles long and the men wore aprons. Mum wore an apron. The men near the door were bigger than the men at the far away end of the counter. There was rows and rows of tins opened so you could see the biscuits inside and the men cut butter with a wire. One of the baddies tried to strangle Ringo with a wire.

 I put the book in the box on the counter. When I was wee I thought it was a magic box. You put your book in the top and on the other side of the counter the book was on the bottom. If you had an orange book and everybody else had a green one you could watch it going doon, doon, doon on our side of the counter. Bert worked in the sosh. He always winked at me. There was sawdust on the floor and sometimes there was footprints going out the shop and along the pavement outside. One of the men shouted, Mrs McCrandle. She was next to be served. Her book had reached the bottom. The men behind the counter made the wifies in the shop laugh. They said things that weren't funny but it still made the wifies laugh.

 Bert made the wifies laugh when he put on a red nose like a clown. I went to smell the cheese. There was one with blue bits in it and Tommy Bruce said he saw a worm in it once. Some of the cheeses were like wheels and when the man cut them you just got a wee bit. One of the cheeses was red. A big red ball. I've never saw red cheese when it was cut. Next to the cheese was the butcher's counter. There was animals hanging on hooks with no skin. One of them looked like Emmy, Geordie's cat. Another man shouted, Mrs Coutts.

 I went back to my seat but it wasn't there. Mrs Blacklaw had taken it. She took Mrs Coutts's as well. Mrs Blacklaw was fat and she had a beard and she blew out her mouth like the wind up a close. She always had her stockings rolled doon to her sandshoes and she had blue legs. I didn't like Mrs Blacklaw. She smelt like a lavvy and she didn't speak to me unless I was with Mum. Mum had said to mind the coupons. Where were the coupons? I put my hand in

THE RINGO KID

my pocket. The one with no hole. I took out my whistle and tennis ball and crocodile and the line with the messages on it and cigarette cards. I had one of Billy Steele, and a lump of chewing gum that Mum didn't allow me to chew. Where were the coupons? Oh I needed the lavvy. If I didn't have the coupons I couldn't get the messages and mum would be crying again.

Ringo McCallum. Everybody in the sosh looked at everybody else in the sosh. So did the men behind the counter. I looked over and saw Bert standing beside the book box. Ringo McCallum he shouted again but even louder now. He wasn't looking at me but all around him. It was like he was saying to everyone, has anybody seen Ringo McCallum? He had our orange book in his hand and I could see the coupons sticking out of one of the pages. I kept my eyes on my shoes when I walked to the bit of the counter that Bert had moved to and put my line on the counter. He said OK Ringo what can we do for you today? He went away with the line and every time he came back he brought something else with him. He got sugar then potatoes then jam then flour then biscuits. I thought he had made a mistake cos they were chocolate biscuits. Mum didn't buy chocolate biscuits unless it was Christmas or something. When he was finished he put the messages in the bag and wrote something in the book and said, OK Ringo see you tonight at the OK Corral and gave me a sweetie. I put the handles of the bag through my arms so it hung on my back and walked out the door with my spurs jangling and my hands just clear of my guns. I liked Bert.

When I got home the house was busy. Mum and Betty were cleaning things and the wireless was on and I was told to go and play. I saw Billy in the backs and went to play with him. There was a big boulder near the shelter and Billy was digging around it with a spoon. A bent spoon. I went up to the house and asked Mum if I could get a spoon. She said no. Geordie's Mum was in the house. Mum asked me if I wanted to go to the pictures with Geordie. And Billy I said. No with Geordie she said. Then I had my tea. Nobody else had their tea just me. Not Mum not Betty not Jimmy just me. I had to eat it at the bunker next to the main. Mum told me to wash my face and wait for Geordie to come. The table was being set with cups and things. I saw the chocolate biscuits from the sosh. Betty was making sandwiches with cheese and ham. The cups were the pink ones with the green flowers. I remember them when Dad left and at Christmas. On the table was a plate covered with a big white sheet. When Mum wasn't looking I lifted up one of the corners of the sheet. Cakes! Cakes with cream and chocolate and lemon and jam. Put that doon said Mum and skelped my hand but not sore.

Geordie came to the door and we went up to the pictures. Geordie was awfy quiet. It was John Wayne. I was still thinking about these cakes when the picture started. He was in Hireland and he wanted to get married but this big really big man said no so they started to fight. He fought in the house and the street and the pub and the fields and he won cos he was a boxer before he wanted to get married. Once I looked at Geordie and he was crying. I looked back at the picture cos I didn't want Geordie to see me seeing him.

Mum wasn't at the close when we got back. I could see the light was on when I got to the top of the stairs and it was quiet. I heard quiet voices in the house and Bert was there and Jimmy and Betty and mum and a man that looked like Bert and a wifie. Bert said, hi Ringo, and everybody laughed. The man laughed like Bert. I looked at my shoes. Mum came and lifted me up. She was happy. She was happy cos it was Saturday.

SCRATCHING THE SURFACE

Ward McGaughrin

I blend in. Like Parmesan into bolognaise. It's an art, an act, a necessity. It's how I survive. I blend in because people either don't look, look away or look right through me. To them I'm just another bit of litter in the wind, which is how it has to be right now.

You might not think it but winter's easier. It gets dark earlier so I merge like a long forgotten memory into the tombstones of the Howff. I've no camouflage, I just am. I got used to the cold. I had to.

Somebody once said people never look up. Believe me, they never look down either. I never did, not this far. I never thought I'd have to. I looked ahead but never saw this life ... if you can call it a life. People say "Life's hard". Compared to what? What else do we know? What can we compare it to? Death?

Sleep's what you worry about first, not food, or even being moved on under Section Blah Blah Blah. There's always food somewhere: bins, skips, even pavements. You can stay up late and scavenge discarded chips or kebabs if you feel exotic. Anyway you can go without food for a couple of days, but sleep – that's a different story.

Deprive people of their sleep and they will tell you all their secrets, all the details you want to know; and the best bit is they're so wrecked they'll think the information's still locked away inside their heads. You need your sleep to function. I know this from experience. Sleep is what I dream about.

But it's not all bad. I have learned patience, because I have had the time. I blend in. You won't find me, so don't try. No-one can. That's not a challenge by the way, it's just a fact. By the time you're read this I'll have moved on. I will be somewhere else. I am aiming for that better place again. A place with the people I remember and loved. I'm itching to get back – literally. How many gravestones say, "Gone but not forgotten"? I am not ready to be forgotten, because I haven't forgotten how I arrived at destination destitute. Or who put me here.

The Howff – a place of the dead – is, ironically, also a meeting place. See that guy there on his mobile phone? Does he know that Dundee's Nine Trades officially began meeting at the Howff in January 1581? I don't imagine tradesmen back then had conversations too different from today. Cloth-cutting, cost-cutting, standards, competition and taxation, all topics shared down through the years.

This one guy's a regular in my al fresco boardroom. Swaggers in like he owns this place. Property developer, landlord, money lender, drug dealer, call him what you will, he's all of the above. Most people don't have a good word for him. I do: scum. Japanese phone in left hand, French fag in the other. Hand made Italian leather shoes and a very expensive Swiss watch. He's a real geography lesson or maybe he's just multicultural. He's known as 'Lord Lucan', but I can find him anytime I want. I could set my watch by him every day ... if I had a watch.

As far as he's concerned that tree belongs to him for the time he's here, same spot, same time. And from what I hear he's on the phone to the same guy every day.

"Jimmy Boy! How ya doing the day? What's on offer t' yer old pal?"

He knows me. He just doesn't recognise me – yet. He's looked right at me when I've approached him before. I'm invisible. He sees a tramp and I see red. But that changes today. Now.

The workies are away for lunch; picks and shovels and a few wooden stakes are just invitations. Probably wouldn't take more than one short sharp shock and that would be it. Over. But I deserve better and he needs worse.

I've rehearsed this in my head every day this week. I've paced it out and practised slowing down my breathing. But right now the entire world is silent, except for my heart.

"Naw, Jimmy Boy, it's too much. I could buy it in a shoap for the same price." His phone buzzes with interference and he turns to get a better signal again. "Bloody mobiles, hing oan."

Here goes. "Heh?" We're face to face.

"Piss aff, ya Jaikkie. Naw, no' you Jimmy Boy, there's some vermin here needs treatment. Haud oan."

I hold his eye and watch his face drain as he looks and eventually sees me.

"Bet you thought you'd seen the last of me. Are you looking at a ghost

SCRATCHING THE SURFACE

in a graveyard? Do the dead keep you awake at night? 'Honest, ah'll git ye yir money, just gie wa' anithir chance' sound about right? You do believe in ghosts, don't you? Of course you do. Otherwise you wouldn't be seeing your 'spookie woman' every couple of weeks."

"Jimmy Boy, get your team down here now. Naw, dinnae feck aboot. I don't care. I said *now*."

"As expected. Big Shot needs someone else, again. Same as you always do. Just like the night of the fire all over again. Remember? An old Victorian ballroom empty and alone, surrounded by derelict tenements and dirt. Remember whose palms you greased to buy it in the first place? And then there was a wee helping hand for planning permission to turn it into a state of the art nightclub – which we both know was never going to open. I'm sure you found them very co-operative. Very talkative in fact. That was their big problem, and now it's yours.

"And then we had your almost passable impression of a proper businessman. What was it you said? Ah yes: 'Not only great for the city, but great for Scotland.' Pure one hundred per cent bullshit."

I've seen his look too many times to be fooled by it. The forced blank stare, head slightly tilted in denial. He knows exactly what I'm talking about.

"Listen pal, ah've nae idea who you are or whit yer oan aboot. Jist' dae yirsel a favour an' scram before the boys get here."

"What, the Tweedle Twins? They messed up big time that night, probably before and since as well. Relatives eh, who would have them? They're the ones you can thank for me surviving that fire. What did they tell you? 'He wis deid when we left him in the cellar, he's jist ashes noo.' Sound familiar?"

This is the first time I've ever seen him stuck. He knows about revenge, he's taken dozens of people out of circulation without batting an eyelid. He's clocked the shovels. They're only just beyond his reach. He's imagining what would happen if he was in my position. A couple of blows for a starter and make a meal of it later – completely.

"Your car was unlocked yesterday morning wasn't it? That makes three times this week. How did that happen, I wonder? Isn't it funny the nightclub electrics have failed completely on one single day this year and last year … and both times on the same date as that big "unfortunate" fire. What does Spookie Isa have to say about that? Did you ask her about why all the carp in your ornamental pond turned green and died?"

"Like ah said, ah don't know you fae Adam."

"Don't bother denying it, your little empire's about to come crashing down around you. I'm just scratching the surface of what's in your future." Traffic noise returns again as my heart rate gets back to normal. There's a new sound, panting and wheezing.

"The Tweedle Twins. Out on your own again boys? Things are looking up."

"Grab that bastard."

They're not bright but they are big. Doormen as big as the nightclub doors they stand in front of. The small one, he's probably only an XXL, lunges full force and knocks me off balance. I grab the back of his collar as we both spin and head for the dirt. I'm up first.

The Aberdeen Angus he came with moves quicker than a man that size should and I'm on the ground again. They both pick me up and I'm held fast between them down on my knees and bent forward.

"Not so smart now are you Martin, ya dick? You blew it back then and you've messed up now."

The Twins pull me backwards as I yell desperately, "I'm not alone."

"Aye right."

"Look around you. See that workie in the van reading the paper, the hoodie smoking a fag at the railings ... "

He hesitates as he checks them out one by one. The van door closes, the alarm bleeps 'on' and bluff number one evaporates.

"Wan doon and wan tae go, then ... "

All eyes on the hoodie as his fag hits the dirt and he hits the road. Not how I had imagined the day.

"An I suppose ye're gonna tell me that wee lassie oan the bench is wae you an'a. Well yer up the creek, pal. That's just Mindless Maggie. She's wan o' mah mules and aboot mah best customer an' a'. She's sprawled oot, aff her face because ah just sold her a big load of smack yesterday. If you're gonny bluff, at least pick a decent hand. Try this wan."

I say nothing. I don't have a chance. His right hook stings far more than my failed bluff.

"Just my luck picking someone you sell drugs to, eh?" I spit out my next words mixed with blood and saliva. "That can't be very many people."

SCRATCHING THE SURFACE

"Heh, smart Alec, a bit o' respect there, please. Ah've lost mair money runnin' for the bus than you ever made in a month. But yer right aboot wan thing, ah've goat a hale empire of customers and they're a' just waiting for a supply coming off the bus in hauf an oor ... in full view o' plod. It's been workin' a dream fir years an' some wee dick like yoo's no gonny stop me."

Right now, he owns the word 'smug'.

"Aw, look at that. Wee Maggie's come tae jine us. How ya dain' doll?"

"Is that right?" I try to control my voice. "Maybe you don't know your Maggie died from contaminated smack this morning. Maybe Daft Billy's going to turn up ... and what about Bullets, or Toke? You must want to see them again ... their grubby wee paws must have paid for a least a couple of houses for you. After all it's only polite to say 'Thank you', isn't it? Maybe they already whisper to you at night. You are not going to rest in peace anytime soon."

The colour drains from his face. "Whit the fu ... ?"

The Tweedle brothers take one look at him, loosen their grip on me, and leg it. You scare more easily if you have just a bit of belief. Enough to have a planted thought grow into a mature torment at what the shadows conceal.

"Git back here ya bastards."

"Now it's two down and one to go – straight to Hell. You'll be able to talk to Spooky Isa anytime you want, from there."

He's stuck for the second time.

"When you look over your sore shoulder, I'll be standing right in front of you. You're going to be surrounded by me and the ghosts of Billy and Maggie and Bullets and Toke and all your other nameless victims. Until I say."

Before I blend in again, he needs to know I'm serious. I use a wooden stake like a baseball bat and crash it into his left clavicle. And vanish.

LOCATION – FIFE

END OF THE LINE

Joyce McKinney

In 1963 we made our last journey to Elie on the train. The paint was fresh on the station's waiting room doors and windows, and the hanging baskets swung gently, still dripping from the evening's watering. The brakes screeched and doors were flung open before we drew to a halt and the children and dogs jumped down onto the platform to disappear into a cloud of steam from the engine.

The station master moved up and down through the crowd as we gathered our belongings, greeting us all by name and shouting at the porters to help with the luggage. Husbands made for the van at the rear of the train to see to off-loading the trunks. The boys were hailed by friends who had arrived earlier – it was quite an event meeting the evening train.

"Where's Tom?" someone called, and he appeared with his barrow, muttering under his breath, hanging back as usual until he was missed and then in no hurry for he was in control. No-one could move until he got there to pile the baggage onto his barrow and then wheel it out slowly to the waiting cart. His half-smoked cigarette was behind his ear and just visible below his blue British Rail cap.

He had begun to walk unsteadily during the last few years, dragging one foot and leaning heavily on the handles of his trolley. When he had nothing on which to support himself he swung his arms in a strangely uncoordinated fashion and it had become difficult to get more than the odd word out of him. He was rather a sad figure, a bit untidy, his once-smart jacket stained and trousers frayed.

"Why don't you take a holiday, Tom?" my husband had once asked him and he had replied, "Ach no-o-o, a'm jist waitin' for the hearse."

Yet a few summers ago he had shouted at us all as we arrived, "Well, here you are back again but I've been there, seen it all – Macchu Pichu, Foothills of the Himalayas, Kanchen Junga, Lake Naivasha."

END OF THE LINE

We knew Tom never left Elie and had worked at the station since he left school, so where had he got all those ideas? The townsfolk kept an eye on him, seeing that he got a parcel at Christmas and left-over cakes from the Charity coffee mornings, for he had a sweet tooth. He was prone to bouts of bronchitis so someone always sent for the doctor to find out if things were all right when he was not at work. There was a tale that he had suffered from athlete's foot and the doctor had said, "Get some air about your feet, Tom." So he had appeared at the station in his socks. Everyone thought his shoes must have worn out and so many pairs of footwear were delivered at his house that the Salvation Army van had to come and take some of them away for distribution elsewhere.

He was physically strong, however, now heaving the trunks onto the back of the cart and calling out their destinations as he did so. "Kirklea, Seaham, The Rocks, East Lodge." Each piece was clearly labelled and Cairter Allen paid no heed in any case, standing stolidly by the horse's head until everything was on board and he could drive off to leave each family's belongings on the appropriate doorstep.

"Thanks, Tom, see you later," the boys shouted as we set off to walk up the street. He only grunted in reply, leaning on his barrow, resting after his efforts, his pockets bulging with the packets of cigarettes he had been given as tips. He was generous with his cigarettes so the station waiting room was a favourite howff.

The children had arrived at the house before us and the door stood open. We could hear them upstairs in their rooms calling to each other and no doubt hauling last summer's books and games out of the cupboards. We retrieved the garden seat from where it had been blown into the flower bed over by the wall and put it back in its usual place under the dining room window. Then we sat for a while listening to the noise of the sea and the gulls and contemplated a garden which had been quite overrun by sand which blurred the edges of the flower beds and buried the struggling roses.

I kicked off my shoes and stretched my legs, pulling the skirt of my frock up above my knees. Evening, and no noise of traffic or hurrying footsteps on city pavements. We were conscious of the quiet, of the huge expanse of sky and the sudden lack of any need to hurry over anything. The other coast could seem very near on clear summer evenings with Arthur's Seat and the Castle

Joyce McKinney

Mound standing dark against the Pentlands.

I stepped into the porch and enjoyed the coolness of the tiles under my feet, then the warmer feel of the wooden floor of the hall. I loved that smell, slightly fusty, of furniture polish and dust, of a house that had been closed up for months. It would disappear in a day or two when the windows had been opened and the air had been allowed to blow through the place.

It never took long to adjust to this other life. In a week my pale limbs had tanned and I felt restored. The children were out of doors from morning until evening, their bikes abandoned where they stepped off them, the garden littered with cricket stumps and balls and with pieces of wood for the tree house they meant to build. Friends came and went and meal times were casual affairs, sometimes eaten outside in the garden or carried down to the beach. On warm evenings we hauled the deck chairs out of the hut and sat in a circle with bare feet in the sand and our supper spread out on the rug.

It was on one of those long light evenings that Tom turned up after supper with a bundle of notebooks under his arm. We'd planned a trip out to the Isle of May for the Tuesday of our last week and it had been arranged that Tom would have a day off work to come with us. He had told the boys he had something he wanted to show them before the trip, for they had spoken about the birds they hoped to see out there. Now he spread his notebooks out on the table in the garden and turned the pages to show us the most amazing collection of notes and neat drawings of birds he had studied, showing their migratory patterns and habitat. We had never seen him so animated and when we exclaimed over the beautiful sketches and he saw how interested we all were he began to tell us how he had borrowed books from the library and found out, firstly about the birds he saw around our own coast, and then about the more exotic birds from other countries. He was especially proud of studies he had made of birds from the Chitwe National Park and of a swirling mass of salmon-pink flamingoes on Lake Naivasha in Kenya. There were detailed watercolours of those and of blue magpie from Kanchenjunga and the chestnut capped-finch from Macchu Pichu. Tom obviously did his own kind of travelling.

The boys had new cameras and the puffins that nested on the island during the summer months were ideal subjects for photography with their

END OF THE LINE

extraordinary face markings and brilliantly coloured beaks. Among Tom's drawings were many studies of those quaint little birds and he told us that he had been out to May Island several times and was keen to show the boys the nesting areas and the best place to see the seals. It was good to see him so keen to share what was obviously a source of great pleasure to him. The boys went to bed excited about the boat trip and I prepared a picnic to take with us. We were to make an early start next morning for the boat left at eight am from Anstruther, a few miles along the coast.

It was just beginning to get light when we were jolted awake by the sirens. It was such an unusual sound in Elie and we could hear voices from the neighbours' gardens and the boys clattering down the stairs and out into the yard.

"It's a fire," they yelled up at us. "We can smell it," and they were off on their bikes before we could stop them. We pulled on some clothes and went outside to find so many of the people we knew out in the street before us.

"It seems to be the station," they told us, and indeed we could see a glow in the sky from that end of the town. A second fire engine screeched round the corner by the church, lights flashing and sirens wailing. We ran with everyone else down along the main street and towards the station.

It was light now. Heavy smoke drifted towards us, and ahead, where the road rose over the railway tunnel, the smoke hung in heavy orange-tinted clouds. As we got nearer we could hear crackling and the shouts of the fire brigade and all was a chaos of hoses and buckets and people milling around, getting in the way as they tried to help. The flames reached high into the sky and the main building, well alight by this time, was engulfed in a searing, roaring mass of fire. Half the roof had gone and more tiles fell as we watched, sending out showers of sparks that threatened to take the fire to the buildings on the other side of the track.

There was nothing we could do. There was no stopping such a blaze; they could only try to contain it and, like us, watch it burn itself out. Bit by bit our station building collapsed until there was nothing left to burn. Only a sooty blackened shell remained and the folk who had been watching eventually began to drift away.

We too wandered slowly homewards, carrying with us the acrid smoky smell which clung to our hair and our clothes. I took a shower, trying to rid myself of the unpleasant reminder of what we had witnessed but it seemed to be everywhere, that heavy reek of burning wood, and I could still hear the exploding glass and the crash of falling roof timbers.

There was no more talk of a trip to the island and just the previous day getting out there before the puffins migrated had seemed to be all important. We hung around the house and garden, appalled at the destruction of something we had regarded as a permanent part of the town. We felt uneasy, anxious when rumours of arson circulated. Little knots of people stood around outside the fruit and vegetable shop and the Post Office, discussing the turn of events. The police were interviewing railway employees they whispered. Several of the men we knew were taken off to the Police Station for questioning. Tom was one of them and we waited anxiously to hear that he had been allowed home.

We knew that he had said all sorts of rash things after the fire and when the police took him off for questioning people told us he had shouted that Mr Beeching would be saved a lot of trouble now we had no station left to be closed down, that we could take care of our own affairs in Elie and didn't need outsiders giving us orders. He was away for some time.

Things changed when the station had gone. The line had been due for closure along with most of the small stations in our area. The men who had been employed there stood around the street corners or sat on the wall down by the harbour. They seemed to have nothing much to do but plenty to talk about. A couple of them found work with the owner of the pleasure boats that were busy enough while the weather was fine and the holiday makers were still around.

Tom became a town worthy, lying on the grass on the Toll Green in the summer and the council men who came to cut the grass ran their machines around him where he lay. We greeted him as we passed but we never regained any kind of intimacy with him for he tended to shun any conversation that involved more than a few words.

There was never any answer as to who had started the fire. Perhaps it had been an accident. Who knows? If people had ideas about who might have done it nothing was ever proved.

Just the two of us return for the funeral. The boys are married and have their

END OF THE LINE

own children now. They often go abroad for holidays although they do come occasionally to our house on the beach in the summer.

It is a cold January day and blasts of hail, rain and wind off the sea strike us with all their force, for the cemetery stands unprotected on higher ground and we are not best clad for the elements. Out on the Forth, the Isle of May, the Bass Rock and Berwick Law are lost in low cloud. A grave-side burial on such a day does not deter a huge crowd of local folks from more than one East Neuk village. They are dressed in respectable dark suits, white shirts and black ties and huddle round the grave under dripping umbrellas that do little to ward off the biting wind and frequent showers of icy hail. The minister, with bare head and blue-knuckled hands, grasps his Bible and delivers a couple of readings and a prayer and the coffin is lowered into the grave.

A cousin who is unknown to us all speaks of the deceased in quite unrecognizable terms. There is talk of Tom's interest in mineralogy and his collection of garnets found out in the bay beyond the lighthouse. There were letters from the Museum in Edinburgh thanking him for specimens he had obviously donated to them. He had studied the local dialects of the villages of the East Neuk of Fife and spent time with fisher folk who, although they lived within very short distances of each other, had a wide variety of language. We force ourselves to linger awhile for it seems to be over too fast, and we feel we should resist the temptation to scurry away to the relative comfort of our cars.

We want to have a walk before leaving for home but although the rain has stopped there is a cold biting wind. We pull on extra clothes we have brought with us in the car and with heads down we lean into the wind and stride out along the beach towards the harbour. The sand comes swirling towards us, stinging our eyes and our cheeks. The sailing boats have been craned out of the water and sit on dry land with rigging clanking, paint peeling and tarpaulin flapping. The beach has altered, with rocks appearing where there had been none, and erosion of the sandy banks along the coastal path leaves fences dangling out over the sea.

Up near the shops people are in a hurry on this wintry day: no time to chat when the wind is howling round the buildings and summer acquaintances have a moment for only a nod of recognition as they hurry about their business. The staff from the coffee shop huddle in the unsavoury bus shelter to enjoy a cigarette. We feel that something is missing now that Tom has gone. Perhaps we could have a bench on the Toll Green with his name on a brass plaque, but he would have hated that.

We go and take one last look at our house. We wonder if we should sell it now that we all use it so much less often. It is cold and dusty inside, the window obscured by the salt spray. We lock up again and pull the gate shut firmly behind us.

THE BENCH

George Reid

Malcolm crossed the footbridge over the dual carriageway that led to the North West corner of Dunfermline's public park. He entered the open space that he had known as a child just as the midday sun appeared from behind the autumn cloud, briefly casting his shadow across the bush-lined footpath. The dulling murmur of the traffic behind him faded as he walked further away from the bridge.

He was confronted by a twenty foot high marble fountain topped by a light blue squatting lion, presumably weathered brass, that was grasping a shield with what must be the city's crest. On each side of this elegant structure there were long disused water fountains he remembered using as a young boy. The corners were hewn into ornate scrolls reaching upwards to the lion but where there had once been a few steps up there was now a large paved area surrounded by a waist-high wooden fence.

From here he looked across to the grey stone houses beyond whose slated roofs were the stands of East End Park. He remembered when his team beat Valencia. It was a freezing evening and he and his Grandfather had sat in the centre stand, a treat from his Father. What a night it had been. Valencia, and they'd beaten them 6-2 ... Valencia! It was the first time he'd seen a black football player, their centre forward. Huge he was but he wore gloves for protection against the frost.

Malcolm turned towards the shelter a few yards to the South. He could see that it was void of the glass panels and wooden benches that he and a few of his primary school pals had once played on. Graffiti stained the boards that now replaced the glass. Looking down the hill that dominated the park he saw a new children's play area about a hundred yards away. A solitary male wearing an old style black duffle coat sat, oddly still, on one of the few benches there, staring at the empty swings and climbing frames.

Malcolm walked slowly down the damp grass slope keeping his steps short, heel to toe like that wee detective, so he wouldn't slip on his backside. The grass was sprinkled with yellowing and browning leaves that twisted and turned as whispers of wind disturbed their decaying slumber. He glanced across at the man on the bench and saw that a chihuahua wearing a tartan coat was huddled on his lap.

Continuing across a wide tree-lined path that cut the park cleanly in two he could see that only a handful of dog walkers, sprinkled on the criss-crossing paths, had risked the chill of the day. Malcolm headed for the bench at the head of the path that led to the town's small railway station, pulling up the collar of his new wax jacket as a cooling westerly breeze caught the nape of his neck. The smell of clean wax gently wafted past the tip of his nose.

He approached the Victorian style bandstand that stood alone in the centre of an open area with a single path leading towards its small ornate entrance gate. The structure was well maintained and he vaguely remembered the town band playing in the summer months during his childhood. He'd also had his first romantic encounter here – with a girl called Fiona whom he'd walked home after the Easter dance at the ballroom. They'd lain on one of the bandstand's benches. "It's all right, you'll be better next time," she'd assured him.

Soon he reached the sodden grass bank that overlooked the station. The nearby bench was still vacant and he made his way towards it. Glancing up the hill he could see that the man at the play area was still there, looking.

He sat down and found himself remembering the times when he'd played in the park with the lads and lassies. He closed his eyes and the memories came flooding back until suddenly –

"Guffy! Guffy, leave him alone, leave him alone – Guffy!" a shrill female voice called.

Malcolm looked towards the panic and saw a great Rhodesian ridgeback bounding down the path from the bridge towards him, its owner a good distance behind, her arms swinging from side to side making her open jacket flap in time with her stretching strides.

Not being tremendously keen on dogs at the best of times, especially big ugly ones, Malcolm's best options flashed by him. Run and be caught and devoured? Play dead? Smile at the eating machine and kid on that he wasn't scared and speak to it kindly like, 'Nice doggy, nice doggy'?

THE BENCH

Oddly though, the dog wasn't barking. Maybe it was mute? Unlikely. Malcolm saw the dog's tail wag briefly as it slowed to the pace of a stalking lion. It approached him and without a word of command stood in front of him.

"Guffy, no, no, don't, Guffy," the woman pleaded as the clip clop of her light brown knee-length boots quickly grew closer.

Nice doggy, nice doggy. Malcolm thought he could see a glint in the dog's black eyes as it slowly stepped forward until its snout twitched against his left knee and a drool of slaver dribbled from its moist lower jaw onto his shoe. Malcolm chanced a glance and saw the dribble had been replaced by something worse which was seeping between the laces of his now soiled brogues.

"Shit," he murmured. To order indeed.

Looking Malcolm in the eye, Guffy squatted as his haunches quivered and the gentle breeze helped the resulting odour seep towards Malcolm.

"Sorry, very sorry," the plump forty-something said. Her well-worn Barbour fell open as she leant forward to clip the lead onto the now smirking Guffy's collar, revealing a tight-fitting ribbed green cardigan. She wore a red beret at the jaunty angle of a 1930's French whore and green cords were neatly tucked into her boots. "I'm really very sorry, he keeps doing that if someone is sitting alone on this bench. He doesn't do it at the other benches, just this one," she explained, gradually regaining her breath.

"That's all right," Malcolm lied.

She fumbled about her pockets until she produced a green plastic bag that she placed over her left hand. Malcolm gave an involuntary shiver as she bent down and encompassed the sloppy pyramid, then in a well practised dexterous movement motioned it into the bag and swished the top closed, as she stood up, trapping the mess and accompanying stench.

"Alistair is it?" she queried as she offered her hand that clasped the lead, "Sorry I'm late."

"No, actually it's Malcolm," he said with a frown as she withdrew her hand.

"Oh, sorry … eh … I haven't seen you here before. New to the area, are you?"

"No, no, but I've been away for a long time. Haven't really been back to the park since I was a wee boy."

"When I saw you from the top of the path I thought you looked similar to my Graham."

"Your husband?" ventured Malcolm.

"My ex, well not really ex. He had an accident here ... fatal."

"Oh, sorry to hear that," Malcolm said, imagining the commotion and distress that must have been caused in this place of peace and pleasure.

"Lorraine, I'm Lorraine," the woman said as she laid the green bag on the ground and offered her hand again.

Malcolm glanced at Guffy for any sign of disapproval before taking her hand as she sat down beside him. Guffy, now facing towards the station, positioned himself between the two of them before lying down and resting his head on his crossed paws.

"Funny name for a dog, Guffy?"

"Graham's choice ... his dog really. I inherited him properly after Graham's accident."

"I see."

"Just at the bridge." She pointed up the path towards the stone railway bridge that was the southern entrance to the park. "He fell over. Pissed, according to the Police report. Left poor Guffy standing peering over the parapet."

Malcolm looked at the back of the dog's head. Its ears twitched as if commenting on Lorraine's story.

"You'll have realized that he was well named though." She nodded towards the bag.

"Mmmmm," Malcolm agreed.

"I never walked Guffy until Graham died. He's taken me to some strange places, you know, but his performances at this bench are the strangest. I'm sorry to be rude, but are you sure you're not Alistair?"

"Positive."

"I was to meet an Alistair here and I thought you might have been put off by Guffy." She nodded down at the apparently uninterested hound.

"Not me, I'm afraid." Malcolm was feeling more comfortable with her now and added with a smile, "Would I not do then?"

She leant back and gave him a deliberate once over. "Depends on your interests actually."

"Blind date was it?"

THE BENCH

"Well yes, internet actually. Quite embarrassing in fact. I sent him a picture of myself but he didn't send one back to me. Too shy, he wrote."

"Took a chance though?"

"Well I had to, Malcolm. I don't get to socialize much, not with looking after Guffy, and he said he was interested in dogs."

"Sure you have the right place?"

Lorraine pondered. "Yes, definitely. I described the paths and bench exactly in fact. He doesn't come from the town so I was very specific."

Malcolm thumbed towards the play area at the top of the park. "That wouldn't be him up the hill, would it?"

Lorraine stood and looked round. "Where?"

Malcolm looked round and could see the duffle coated figure about to disappear between the trees and bushes at the top of the hill.

"Guy in the duffle coat." He pointed over Lorraine's shoulder getting a pleasant whiff of perfume in complete contrast to the motioning Guffy. "Can you see just at the top of the hill? He's just going. Look."

"Duffle coat?"

"Yes, and he had a chihuahua," Malcolm offered.

"Oh God, I hope he wasn't put off by Guffy here."

"I'm sure he wasn't."

"It probably wasn't Alistair anyway. He didn't mention he had a dog, especially not a Chihuahua."

"It was maybe a surprise."

"It would have been for him, Malcolm. Guffy nearly ate the last chihuahua he met, or so Graham told me. Tried to mount it as well. Very complicated I imagine."

"Very," Malcolm offered.

Lorraine pondered a moment. "Well that's the excitement over for today by the looks. Unless ... ?"

"We can have a chat if you wish," Malcolm, said taking a chance. "I've plenty of time. I was just remembering, before you came along, about how the park was when I was young. My best friend, Robert, and I used to cower behind the parapet of that bridge there when we were trainspotting. That was supposed to offer us protection from the smoke but it never did." Even as he spoke, Malcolm recalled that long forgotten taste and eye-smarting filth.

A solitary young woman with a pushchair strolled past. She was speaking to the young occupant whose pink bobble hat could be clearly seen moving from side to side as if in time with a pipe tune.

"That reminds me of myself," Malcolm said. He'd had a sudden image of himself as a child in his metal-sprung pram, wrapped up against the cold breezes. "If the hood of the pram was up old ladies would probably peer into my warm nest and 'coo coo.' If it was a nice day and I was sitting up they'd give me a slobbery kiss."

Lorraine laughed. "Can you remember that far back?"

"Well, I could imagine that from a photo my mother has of me. I can certainly remember when I got to school age and my Gran's friends got hold of me. Ugh, the taste of stale tea and cakes. I was forever wiping my mouth after those moments. No wonder I've got pyorrhea!"

Malcolm had never found it so easy to talk to anyone. They sat until late afternoon swapping their stories and reminiscences about their upbringing and school days. Finally they swapped phone numbers and e-mail addresses.

"I'll definitely take up that offer of dinner," Lorraine said as she picked up the green bag.

Guffy stood, stretching his front and back legs, his spine visible through his short fur as his back arched under the comforting movement.

Lorraine leant forward and kissed him on the cheek. "Sorry about this again," waving the bag towards the green box at the end of the path. "I'm sure Graham was responsible for teaching Guffy to do that. He could be a devil sometimes."

The dog's head leant towards Lorraine and his ears twitched as if confirming her suspicion. Guffy looked back at Malcolm as they left and he had the impression that the dog kind of approved of him, maybe …

Malcolm started to walk up the hill and they waved to each other as Lorraine and Guffy walked over the railway bridge. Maybe he should think of getting a dog himself? On the other hand, if things worked out he might be walking Guffy soon.

THROUGH A GLASS DARKLY

Amanda Barclay

It's still dark as I park opposite the sea wall. Orange street lights twinkle from across the Forth. Over there, rush hour is just beginning.

The spot I've selected is well out of sight of any security cameras. I carefully check my kit one more time: respirator, head torch, camera, batteries and a few other – ahem – 'tools of the trade'. Fail to plan, plan to fail and all that. Then it's out the car, and a casual stroll back to the inert blackness of the power station.

The 'Heart Attack' snack van nearby is silent and shuttered up. The smell of fried food loiters. I belch gently at the memory of the burger I'd had here just last week. Only just stopped tasting it. Seagulls hunker morosely on the railings, flapping their wings in a half-assed way before they settle back to brooding.

From a discreet distance I check out the Gate House. Sweet. Both Security Guards are safely inside. Better still, they are both fully occupied, slurping Typhoo and struggling with the Teatime Teaser. Just how I like it. A quick skirt round the perimeter fence and I'm in. No need to concern you with how. Just consider it a fait accompli.

As a rule I don't tell people how I spend my days off. Urban exploration is supposed to be secret. I mean it's not a secret society like the Masons; it's more that we don't widely advertise what we do. For the uninitiated Urb-Ex is about exploring those old abandoned buildings that are waiting to be demolished. Have you ever looked at an empty factory wondering what it is like inside? No? It's maybe a Marmite thing. You either get it or you don't. It certainly attracts all sorts. Some people do it for the rush, that thing of being somewhere they shouldn't be. For others it's the whole challenge of infiltrating a site. We never refer to it as trespassing; it's 'infiltration'. It might seem like a strange way to pass the time but any hobby is when you think about it. It's no weirder than potholing, or golf.

Amanda Barclay

For me, it's about finding new places to explore. I like being the first person to get inside and scoop the best photos. There's something strange and beautiful in amongst all that dereliction and decay. It's short-lived and ephemeral. That pause at the end of a working life before the bulldozers blast in.

Methil Power Station has been on the radar for a while. There's been loads of stuff on the forums. So far no one's made it in. This baby is locked down more securely than Fort Knox. The doors are bricked up with steel panels welded on top; then for good measure they've thrown in some serious padlocks. It's understandable – some of the local Neds look on security as some kind of personal challenge. Anyhow I have a good feeling today, like I might just crack this one.

I nip across the staff car park. The empty spaces speak volumes, like chalk outlines at a crime scene. Along the bay to Largo, the sky is softening rapidly to dark blue. I need to keep moving.

Up close, the building is massive. The vast grey trapezium of the turbine hall looms over me. I know exactly where I'm headed.

I'd spent a bit of time here last week having a recce. They say that you always need one way in and two ways out. I was gazing across the burn when an old boy wanders up with a lumpy-looking Lidl bag.

"You a golfer? Do you want to buy a bag of balls?"

I gesture to the binoculars round my neck, and wheel out the cover story I use when I'm scoping a site.

"Nope, I'm a birdwatcher, mate. I passed some angry golfers back there though. They reckon someone's been nicking their balls. If you start running now you'll get a good start."

He laughs wheezily. "Och, these are just lost balls that get washed into the burn. I mind when there was a golf course across there too," he says, nodding at the station.

"Don't tell me. You remember when it was all just fields round here too."

"Well it was, before they built that monster," he says indignantly.

It's hard to imagine something this solid and definite not being there. Mind you, it has those spare lines that just shout Sixties. Did people see it as an eyesore when it was built or as the start of a bright new future?

THROUGH A GLASS DARKLY

Old Father Time has got up a good head of steam now. He points to the cranes, suspended on an elegant colonnade of pillars. The cabin is midway across, paused in space and time.

"See during the miners' strike, that place never stopped. They knew something big was in the offing. You couldn't see daylight between the piles of coal and the crane. No one had ever seen anything like it. In came the coal; out went the miners. That place just kept on running."

I nod absently, hoping he'll take the hint. Instead he takes it as genuine interest and carries on.

"And that artist boy Jack Whatsisname? The one that paints the fancy paintings."

"Jack Vettriano."

"Aye right – I knew him when he was plain Jack Hoggan."

You'd never be allowed to forget your roots here.

"What about him then?" I eventually ask.

"Well, he painted that place. It's alright. If you like that sort of thing. Probably be worth a bob or two after they knock it down."

"That won't be happening for a bit surely?"

"They've got the go-ahead already. My pal's son works for one of the contractors. They start stripping out all the stuff inside a week today."

He's got my full attention now. If I want to see inside it has to be sooner rather than later.

The metal staircase zigzags endlessly all the way up the outside of the building. Time to start climbing. I make for the fire exit that I'd spotted at roof level last week. Best not to look through the gaps in the stair risers. The handrails feel wafer thin and are bubbled with corrosion. Sea air has taken its toll. There's a sharp, sudden pain in my right hand. Bugger. A fragment of rusty metal has become embedded in the flesh between my thumb and forefinger. I pull it out and it starts to bleed.

Getting into the building should be a breeze. It's so high up here you practically need oxygen. Presumably Neds don't have a head for heights as they've gone a lot easier on the security. I start by having a go at the lock. Should be a simple five minute job but fast forward twenty minutes and I'm still faffing round like an amateur. I'm not helped by the spiteful breeze that has picked up from nowhere, numbing my fingers. I eventually opt for a lever and brute force. It's coarse but effective. The door frame eventually splinters and yields. Damp has warped the door which screams in protest as I open it.

Finally I'm in. I don my respirator and head torch. I need to see where I'm going and let's just say between dust, asbestos and the fall-out from roosting birds, it's hardly a walk up an alpine hillside here.

Above my head pigeons chutter quietly, strutting over the skylights. Far far below in a stygian gloom is the main hall. I take stock and try to get my bearings. A bank of filthy glass windows stare blankly in on the hall. That has to be the main control room. Where better to start?

A vast cream console dominates the room. It's futuristic and yet oddly dated at the same time. All warning dials and telephones. All it needs is Homer Simpson eating donuts and hitting random buttons. I get my camera out.

That's when I hear it. It's so faint that you'd hardly notice it. A low murmur like someone chatting in the next room, or machinery running in the distance. Maybe the contractors are making a start ahead of schedule. I step out the office and cautiously check out the hall. There's nothing and nobody there. It could be the sea outside and yet … it doesn't have that gentle steady rhythm of waves.

Next stop is the turbine hall. There's a gloomy chill down here that just seeps into your bones. Lurid green slime patches stain the floor like ectoplasm. The turbines are softly cloaked in matching coats of dust. On one, the viewing hatch is skewed open at a crazy angle, revealing ghostly piles of ash within. Hard to believe this place has only been shut for eight years especially when I spot a fern sprouting jauntily from a control box. Brilliant. It's Urb-Ex shorthand for rot and decay and will make a great photo. I just need to get the exposure right. As I focus my camera, the murmuring noise ratchets up abruptly in volume.

Hours pass as I explore and probe but I keep an eye out for the time. It's all very well getting in under the cover of darkness but I really don't fancy that staircase a second time in the dark. Besides it's hardly a blow getting caught on your way out.

I've left the offices till last. It's pure 'Marie Celeste' in here. It's like the entire staff just pushed their chairs back and left. Files and folders are still strewn across the desks. The calendar on the wall says 'December 1999'.

THROUGH A GLASS DARKLY

Cryptic instructions are scrawled bossily over white boards. 'Remember to purge ancillary tanks in STRICT sequence!!!!!!'; I hope they did remember.

As I lift the camera, there's a movement in my peripheral vision. I spin round. Nothing there. Yet the pages on the staff notice board flutter as if someone has breezed past. An uneasy sensation of being observed trickles down my spine.

I walk across and look more closely at the board. Yellowing charts which had documented the vital statistics of 'Output Power' are now bowed and curled. Swinging forlornly on a single drawing pin, an 'Extraordinary General Meeting' is announced. The agenda reads 'Wind up and Dissolution of Social Club'. Even the fun had stopped. Time to leave.

I start to retrace my footsteps. It's as I pass the turbines a second time that I spot it. I'm not sure why I didn't see it on my way in. Both of the turbines have been numbered with big brass plaques, only the plaque on the Number One Turbine has slipped and is attached by only one screw. A bit of Brasso and that plaque would look dead smart in my flat. A little souvenir of my visit. Now I know that old chestnut about 'taking only photos and leaving only footprints'. All very noble and all that, but ... Next week this is all going to get thrown in a skip anyway. It's not like I'd be actually stealing. In fact, more like preserving for posterity. It's a no-brainer really.

I give the plaque a strong wrench. It comes away with unexpected ease. So unexpected that I fall backwards, landing in a slimy puddle. A sudden draught blows through. It sounds like a sharp intake of breath. Then the murmuring sound gets louder. I'll be glad to get out of here; it's starting to spook me.

It's far worse climbing down the metal stairs than it had been coming up. I can actually see how corroded they are. With every footfall the treads creak alarmingly. I spot the yellow coat of a security guard in the yard below and automatically duck down. This startles a pigeon which suddenly breaks cover and whirls up past my face. I leap back heavily.

Everything happens next in double time and slow motion simultaneously. There's an ominous crack. Then the step just shears and falls away. My right foot flails in fresh air for ever. Somehow I gain purchase with my left. I tumble and thump downwards. My fall is arrested only as I manage to grab a railing at the next landing and catch myself. Panting, I lie there, heart racing. After five minutes I'm still too petrified to move. I swivel my eyes upwards. Where the step had been, there is now only a jagged void. I turn my head carefully and look down to where the security guard had been. He must have heard the commotion. But there's no sign of him. He's either gone for back up or is waiting at the bottom of the stairs. Fan-bloody-tastic.

I've no choice now. I don't care if I do get caught. All I care about is that these stairs hold long enough for me to get down in one piece. Easing myself up, I tentatively test the next step, then the next. Slowly and painfully I pick my way down. Underfoot, rust and debris fall like confetti. That cat on the tin roof has nothing on me. I finally make it to the bottom. Fortunately there's no welcome party to meet me. I sprint to the fence and slip out the way I came in. I look back at the Gatehouse. Odd both the guards are sat inside and neither is wearing a yellow coat.

I trudge back to the car. It's been a day and a half. Pierced hand, wet jeans, oh and the small matter of a near brush with death. Hey ho, I've done it though. I am the first man in and I've got the photos to prove it. I start to plan my trip report to post on the forums. Throwing my kit in the car, I decide to see how the photos have turned out.

The first frame is just a dark square, as is the next and the next. I start to scroll forward frantically. Every frame is the same. No way.

I saw the photos as I took them. Perhaps the fall damaged ... No. wait a minute, here's one. It's of the office but it looks like a double exposure. A man stands by the notice board, arms folded and stares accusingly right at the lens.

The sun is dropping fast. From here, the station dominates the skyline. I lean back in my seat, staring at its menacing dark form. Then suddenly a gleam in my kit bag catches my eye. I get out the car and very deliberately place the plaque on the sea wall. Silhouetted against the flaming sunset, the chimney stack throws a defiant vertical gesture back at me. With a start I see the office windows are ablaze with light. A few moments pass before I realise it's only the winter sun reflecting on glass.

NORA'S GARDEN

Claire MacLeary

In the middle of St Andrews, down a narrow lane, lies a secret garden. There are many such lanes in St Andrews – and many such gardens – remnants of the 'lang riggs' which, in the Middle-Ages, sustained the cattle and the crops of this ancient town's inhabitants.

I lie in bed in the half-light dreaming about gardens. I can see the privet-bound rectangle of my early childhood, orderly rows of carrots, onions, cabbages and cauliflowers, red-currant bushes and raspberry canes. And, look, there's my garden at home – lilacs and roses in scented profusion, a sweeping lawn, a garden seat, a sunhat-shaded baby in a shiny, coach-built pram.

I don't have a garden now, not since I moved from the big house in the country to this flat but, of course, there are compensations. I'm a regular at my Church – a bit of an insurance policy, really – then there's the Library and the theatre. It's called The Byre, and the cinema's called The Picture House. That's *one* thing I should manage to remember!

The shops here are old-fashioned. The newsagent has gold letters up above which still read 'Christian Institute'. Mrs Innes is a pet and invariably asks, "How are you dear?"

"Couldn't be better" I always tell her. (I was brought up not to complain).

The girls at Fisher and Donaldson wear red striped pinnies and straw boaters, and write your bill down in pencil on a miniature pad. I buy a Dr Floyd's loaf once a week and keep it in the fridge. If it's raining I might treat myself to a fudge doughnut or a rhubarb tart. The man in the Meal Shop is *so* obliging. He'll weigh me out two ounces of rough oatmeal or put one Free Range egg in a double brown paper bag. At Birrell the greengrocer down by The Port they have lovely, floury potatoes and fat gooseberries and rasps and, further along South Street in Wilson the ironmonger's, the nice men in their grey coats will cut me a Yale key for £1. I'm always losing my keys these days.

I invariably wake early. I get up and pull the curtains so my neighbours know I'm still alive. Then I make a cup of tea and a slice of toast and tuck back in under the covers with the *St. Andrews Citizen* and my faithful Roberts radio. Sometimes I just lie there, revelling in my good fortune and gazing at the sea.

Mid-morning I venture 'up town' and have a cappuccino at The Doll's House. They have a whole rack of newspapers, so I can read the lot. Of course, once I'm out, I'm out for the day. I organise my shopping first. Sometimes I go to Tesco in Market Street, where I buy my staples, and they pack them in a box for Paul Meldrum to deliver right to my door. Paul says I'm never in, but nobody ever touches them all the same. If I dawdle in the Doll's House and leave it too late, the kids come streaming out of Madras, their white shirts hanging out, ties defiantly at half-mast, and swamp me completely. Once I couldn't move in the bacon aisle for Prince William's security detail. Still, I sleep safe at night with that big, armed policeman walking round the block.

My 'social life' starts at lunchtime. The Coffee House in Greyfriars Garden does a lovely bacon roll, and I'll meet Pat or Margaret or Sheila and have a natter before we go out. On Mondays there's the Ladies Social Club and on Tuesdays there's Haydays at The Byre. I just *love* The Byre! You can paint, or learn drumming, or do calligraphy, or whatever, and there are always lots of young people about to liven things up. They clatter up and down the stairs when we're sitting doing our painting, shouting out about 'Costume' or 'Lighting' or 'Production.' The wee girls at the Box Office are so helpful, and Kate in the Coffee Shop always has time to talk. There's a grand piano downstairs – though I've never seen anyone play it – and sometimes an Art Exhibition, so you can spend all day there, really. Wednesday is my stint at Save the Children. Thursday I have an Art Class at the Memorial Hall, but The Byre is the highlight of my week.

My friend Margaret always comes with me to The Byre. We go to nearly every show there, using our concessions and our 'Friends of the Byre.' We like good plays the best – Chekhov or Pinter or the like – and excerpts from opera. Margaret doesn't see well, so we sit in the front row. In the interval we have a gin and tonic. If we don't like the production, we don't go back in. We just stay in the bar.

Pat and I go together to Arthritis Care. Of course neither of us actually *has*

NORA'S GARDEN

arthritis, but we heard in the Ladies Social Club that Arthritis Care has lovely catering, and wonderful outings in the summer. And the meetings don't last long.

After Church on Sunday, there's tea in the Church Hall, then some of us 'girls' will take a turn along The Scores and have a walk on the West Sands. In the summer we'll play a round of putting on the Himalayas or have lunch at the Links. On a rainy day, we'll go into the Woollen Mill and try on their expensive Avoca tweeds. It's lovely in there – toasty warm, with plush tartan carpets, and even the fitting-rooms are fancy. But, oh, when I look in the mirror these days, I say to myself, "Nora, you're getting *so* thick around the waist. Thank God you've still got your legs!"

Later we might buy a fish supper at Peter Michael's and share it between us, or an ice cream cone at Luvian's, or maybe a nougat wafer to splash out.

The only thing I *really* miss here is my garden. Sometimes I'll sit in St Mary's and watch people picnicking on the grass or have a stroll through the Lade Braes or a wander round the Botanic Gardens, and once a year there's a Hidden Gardens Day, when you can have a nosey in Hepburn Gardens or Dauphin Hill or Ladies Lake but, if I'm at The Byre and the café is busy, I'll go round to a wee bit of waste ground down the lane. It must have been a garden once, for there's the odd bulb in the springtime and rosehips in winter, but it's all overgrown now behind its high, stone wall. I call it my 'secret garden' for I can sit there on a summer's day imagining what life was like here centuries ago. I just love that little space! Nobody ever bothers me there, and I can sit in the sun with my back against the wall just day-dreaming, or else planning in my head the most wonderful, scented garden for future generations to enjoy.

I did once speak to one of the girls at the Box Office – Jennifer, I think she's called, though I get them a bit mixed up.

"Do you know who owns that bit of waste ground down the lane?"

"I think it belongs to The Byre, but I'll check for you".

Some days later: "Hello, Nora. Yes, I *did* ask, and the garden *does* belong to The Byre".

"Garden," I say. "That's stretching it. It's completely overgrown."

"Well, I know, but, you see, we just haven't the funds."

That's a bit feeble, I think. Surely such a vigorous, young bunch could soon raise some cash. But I nod sympathetically and say "Thank you" nicely and, for once, bite my tongue.

But, over the coming weeks, I think and think about my secret garden until, one day at The Byre, I collar the Marketing Manager.

"Why don't you do something about that piece of waste ground down the lane?"

"Well, we would love to, but the Arts Council has withdrawn its funding this year, so there are no spare funds."

"Surely it wouldn't cost a lot," I retort. "It's a pretty small space. All it would take is a bit of landscaping and a few shrubs."

"I quite agree. There were even plans drawn up a few years ago, but they've been mothballed."

"Perhaps you could dig them out again," I say coyly.

"I'll have a look."

Next time I'm in The Byre I knock on his office door.

"David? Remember me? Did you ever find those plans?"

"Plans? What plans?"

"Plans for the disused garden."

"Oh, yes, I *did* find them. They're somewhere in this pile."

The plans are faint photocopies of what looks like an architect's drawing, but I can make out a semi-circular amphitheatre with stepped stone seating fronted by a paved 'stage'. An area of lawn is bordered by shrubs, and climbing plants soften the high stone wall.

"Oh!" I exclaim "It's just beautiful! Wouldn't it be marvellous to make it actually happen?"

"Well, of course it would. We're so tight for space here. We could use it for all sorts of things – poetry readings, Haydays, story-telling, Youth Theatre. But … the Board is adamant that there are just no funds."

That night, in bed, my mind races with the possibilities of that sorry, unkempt space. Eventually I fall asleep, dreaming fitfully of my secret garden.

I don't get much mail these days, nothing but bills, but next day I do get a letter. It's from the doctor's surgery. They want me to make an appointment for a 'routine check-up.' I wonder what that is? To be honest, I don't really fancy it, but I suppose they'll only pester me if I *don't* go. So I make an appointment with Doctor Nelson and take a taxi to the surgery in Pipeland Road – I'm geed up enough at the very thought of a doctor without having to arrive out of

NORA'S GARDEN

puff! That nice Doctor Nelson says my blood pressure is sky-high. I give him my best smile and say, "Well, Doctor Nelson. It's a long time since I've been alone in a room with a handsome young man." Then I say, "Why don't we just sit and chat for a while, and then you can take my blood pressure again?"

So he does that – and it *is* much better. I *knew* it would be better when I calmed down! Then the doctor says, "All the same, Nora, I would like you to take an aspirin every morning. That will help to stop you falling over."

I *knew* I shouldn't have told him about falling over. Not tripping, you understand, just keeling over. Mind you, St Andrews is breezy. One day I even had to hang onto a lamp-post by Hope Park Church it was blowing such a gale.

All of a sudden I am lying in the half light again, dreaming about gardens. I can see the tidy vegetable plot of my childhood, the sumptuous garden of my marital home, a walled garden down a narrow lane. I glance around. A strange bedside table sits by my bed. There's no sign of my library book – and where *is* my Roberts radio? Am I back in my old house?" I wonder. "Did I *really* move to that flat in St Andrews?

I rack my brains. Perhaps I've been having a nightmare – or maybe I just dreamt it all. But, no. I'm *sure* that there was a castle – and a cathedral – and a secret garden.

Then I realise that my bedroom seems awfully dim. Oh dear, I think. I must have forgotten to pull the curtains. Next thing there's a strange man in the room. He's wearing a white coat, and I realise he's speaking to me.

"Nora? Can you hear me, Nora?"

Well, of *course* I can hear him! (He's speaking quite loudly.)

"Nora," he's saying now, "can you move your right arm for me, Nora?"

"*Move?* My right *arm?*"

And now I'm right up on the ceiling. And I'm floating. And there are all these strange people crowding round my bed. And I can see the whole of St Andrews – the castle, the cathedral, the houses, the gardens.

And look! There's The Byre. And there's my secret garden. It's been landscaped like a little amphitheatre and laid to lawn and shrubs. There's a silver birch tree in one corner, and sweet-scented roses are climbing over the old stone wall. I can see figures moving, and hear children's voices. Imagine! The Byre Youth Theatre is rehearsing there!

In the middle of St Andrews, down a narrow lane, lies a secret garden. There are many such lanes in St. Andrews – and many such gardens. It takes just a few moments to sit quietly and imagine the 'auld grey toon' as it was when the buildings were made of wood, and pilgrims and scholars and merchants from the Low Countries beat a path to the Cathedral and the University and the Mercat Cross. And, if you are ever in St. Andrews, and you manage to find such a garden, you never know, you just might see me too.

CAST ADRIFT

Stuart Wardrop

Dry lightning flickered on the horizon beyond the dimly illuminated Forth Railway Bridge and thunder muttered uneasily beyond Inchcolm as the old Volvo wheezed and clanked into the residential street behind the foreshore. Duggie glanced at the dashboard clock – seven pm and already dark. No moon or stars tonight and an overcast sky – ideal, provided he could see the target from wherever he could park this load of crap.

He passed the house on Battery Road, did a three pointer further up the street and came by the house again. Pitch black. No – a chink of light at the front window – must be the living room. Tonight might not be a waste of time then, not like the past three nights when he had sat on his backside for hours watching nothing happening.

Duggie wrestled the Volvo into a different spot tonight, between the sea wall and the Albert Hotel. It wouldn't do to arouse the suspicions of some sad old bastard with nothing better to do than look out the window. Not bad – he could see the front of the house and had a good enough view of the street.

He cranked down his window to let the cigarette stink out and wrinkled his nose as the rankness of the bay rushed in. What the hell possessed this guy to live here – or anywhere else in North Queensferry for that matter? The tide was out and the air hung heavy with the sickly stench of salt and slimy seaweed.

He wound the window up, made himself as comfortable as he could in the cramped driver's seat and settled to a vigil that would probably last until midnight. Mind you he would bill it as ending at four am – and for a few days more than it took. Got to make a living somehow and this client seemed rich enough and eager enough for a result not to fuss over details – provided he delivered.

Anyway, he thought, I've had so much bloody bad luck it's about time the tide turned. He winced at his choice of words.

It was true though. Everyone thought that being a private investigator was romantic and rewarding – all Sam Spade, whisky and meaningful looks from sultry blondes. In fact Duggie's life largely consisted of long boring periods punctuated by even longer boring periods. He had piles, chronic indigestion, an overdraft and precious little else. And he drank too much.

Even what he had was about to go down the tubes. Most of his living, if you could call it that, came from taking statements for legal firms – precognitions they were called. This had dried up, partly because of a change in the system but mainly because he had fallen out big time with a snooty little bitch of a lawyer who had put the word about around her pals that Duggie took shortcuts and that his bills were iffy.

Typical of the way his luck was going. The bank was pushing again and even the antique he was sitting in was up for repossession. Bloody good job the house was in Sandie's name – a present from her dad – along with the regular handouts that he wasn't supposed to know about.

Duggie shifted in his seat and lit a cigarette. He'd been lucky to land this client. His thoughts wandered to the good looking and obviously well-heeled forty something trying, with more than a touch of desperation, to pass herself off as a good-looking and well-heeled thirty something. She was divorcing her husband, the guy in the house by the bay, but reckoned that he was seeing another woman. As they were getting divorced anyway Duggie couldn't see much point in pursuing this but it was to do with beefing up the divorce settlement. In any case she was the client; the client was always right and he had no problem in doing his own bit of fleecing. In Duggie's world there was always room for one more snout in the trough and no reason why it shouldn't be his.

Quarter to eight. Light still leaked from the front window curtain but there was nothing to see and the street was dark and as quiet as the grave. God, he thought, I feel like the only man on earth. Ironically the rumbling echo of a northbound train on the bridge only reinforced this feeling of emptiness.

As the echo faded Duggie lit another cigarette and debated about coffee or a swig from his flask. Too early for coffee. It would go straight through him and though the chance of police interest was remote he didn't want to smell of booze if that happened.

As he drew on his cigarette and relaxed as much as the lumpy seat would allow Duggie knew what would happen next. It always did when he let his mind idle in neutral. He couldn't stop it and wasn't sure that he wanted to.

Eyes closed, his thoughts drifted as the familiar memories began to thread through his consciousness, like old and not always welcome friends.

He had quite liked school really and was anything but stupid. Teachers didn't seem to notice though. Too busy fawning over the rugby and cricket kids – bloody teachers' pets. These thickos could do no wrong. This puzzled him for a bit but then he decided that teachers simply had a down on him – their loss.

He opened his eyes. Christ – something was going down and he had almost missed it. A car had stopped outside the house – a taxi. A figure stooped at the driver's window then a long raincoat scuttled up the path – yellow light leaping out the front door. Can't watch raincoat and taxi both, he thought. He couldn't see the number but clocked that it was an Ace Taxi.

By the time he had refocused it was too late. The raincoat was through the door, the door was tight shut and the path dark and silent. Sod it. Absolutely bloody typical. With a proper team he would've got IDs on the woman – if it was a woman – and the taxi. Still – there would be another chance when she came out.

Settling down again, he picked at the scab of memory. Yes, people had a bit of a down on him. He no longer bothered with reasons. This was why he'd bounced from job to job after leaving school and it even pursued him into the army. He reckoned he was doing quite well there before he'd had to carry the can for the business with the Iraqi prisoners and they chucked him out – public school mafia bastards. One of them had the cheek to describe him as well-balanced – a chip on each shoulder. The whole thing was so bloody unfair and civvy street was no sodding different.

Jeez this is boring, he thought. My arse hurts and I'm beginning to need a pee. Maybe I could use the pub toilet. No, not a good idea. Another train rumbled overhead. Perhaps he could count the trains to pass the time. The house remained dark and quiet. Whatever they're doing they were taking their bloody time about it. He looked at his watch. Half past eight. God, hours to go. A wee nip would do no harm, but no coffee, not with his bladder the way it was. Only ten fags left – have to ration them if these buggers down there didn't get on with it.

Things had looked a shade more promising when Sandie's dad found him a job in his recycling firm. Duggie had reckoned that dumping crap wasn't rocket science and had privately felt that it was a waste of his talents. He'd made some improvements and felt that he was doing well. It didn't last though and in echoes from the past he'd found himself being blamed for things that weren't his fault. Then the bastards had made him redundant. They'd given him some cash, not as much as he deserved, but advice from a so-called financial advisor had left him a year later with barely enough to set himself up as an investigator working from home. Now it looked like circumstances were conspiring to bugger this up as well.

Duggie occasionally had flashes of insight into his life but he remained firmly convinced that things would get better – thanks to Sandie. She kept a hostile and malignant world at bay and steadfastly refused to say, or hear, a word against him.

What was it that butler guy said about Diana? He was her rock? Well Sandie was his rock and she could always find a solution that made him feel good about himself. At the same time, he reasoned, she was his wife; supporting him was in her job description.

Mind you, she didn't know the bit about the bank and the car repossession. He reckoned though that when he told her she wouldn't moan on about it. She would work it out and everything would be okay. Thinking about her cheered him up. Another nip would hit the spot and it was time he had one of his fags.

A sudden flurry of movement startled him. Duggie looked round in panic to see a bunch of dark shapes milling around outside the Albert. He slid as far down the seat as he could and held his breath as one of them urinated for what seemed like forever against the sea wall just by the Volvo. Duggie sneaked a look at his watch. Of course, this was the Albert chucking out time. Maybe he could have chosen a better parking place.

He shuddered at the thought of some drunken bugger trying to steal his car – or challenging him, in that single-minded way that drunks have, about why he was sitting there in the dark.

He released pent up breath as the shouting and laughter faded and in his mirrors he saw the Dunfermline bus leaving the bus stop on the Town Pier outside the pub and a small group of men heading noisily for the Brae leading to the upper part of the Ferry.

CAST ADRIFT

Dark silence again reigned outside the Albert and Duggie saw that it had begun to rain. He returned his gaze to the target and just as he was beginning to nod off an Ace taxi pulled up at the kerb and the path was suddenly bathed in yellow light. A figure – no – two figures were separating on the doorstep. The long raincoat fluttered down the path and the taxi moved off.

The Volvo spluttered and groaned into life after only two goes. "There is a God," Duggie muttered. He pulled out carefully and followed the taxi, worn wipers smearing and squealing across the windscreen. He had to keep his distance though, at this time of night, there was not much on the Old Road to Inverkeithing.

The next bit was easy. All he had to do was follow the taxi and get the address. Tomorrow he would look up the Electoral Roll, confirm, using the salesman trick, construct an imaginative report and collect the fee. Nothing to it really. He felt his spirits soar. Things were definitely looking up.

Hang on though. Something wasn't right. This … this was all wrong. The taxi's slowing, indicating left, pulling into the kerb. What the … The raincoat turned away and floated up the path triggering the security light. The taxi pulled away and the security light died as the door closed.

Christ, Duggie thought – did all that just happen? He remained where he had stopped four or five houses away. A pinprick of pain at the back of his head blossomed into a fireball that threatened to explode from his skull. His white-knuckled hands gripped the steering wheel and his breath caught in his chest. Nausea rose in his throat and sweat prickled his forehead, running in scalding streams down his face and back.

He stared unseeingly at the windscreen for a full ten minutes. Disjointed thoughts swarmed and struggled in his brain like drowning swimmers, none making an ounce of sense. Then they stopped struggling and sat watchful on the sidelines. The nausea receded, his hands relaxed and the pain in his head subsided to a dull throb.

No need to check with Electoral Registration or for the salesman bit. There would be no client report either – padded or otherwise. Because Duggie knew exactly who lived in that house.

THE CHALLENGE

Paul Sykes

It was a typical Fife night in January – wet. Travis Milne, ensconced in the Howe of Fife rugby clubhouse, looked up from his dog-eared copy of *The Sandman* and eyed the television miserably as Sky Sports News endlessly looped the same dreary stories. He wondered how the network penetration test was going and glanced at his Blackberry. The week had been a long one and the client a nightmare. Travis weighed up his options: have another drink or go home. No point in going home to drink alone; he sluiced down the best part of half a pint and rolled over to the bar. The faded images of teams of smiling Cupar menfolk bore down on him.

At the end of the bar stood a group of middle-aged men. At the epicentre was a man in his early thirties, with silver-flecked blond hair and a face the colour of claret. Travis scowled at him. Torquil Farquar had been lecturing loudly about the joys of golf. Travis hated golf and he had been force-fed a lifetime's trivia in the last hour. He now knew why links were superior to parkland courses, why Prestwick out-ranked the Old Course and every feature of the new TaylorMade irons and, to cap it all, Torquil frequently referred to the game as *gowf*, which made Travis' teeth fur over.

"Do you know the word 'golf' is actually an acronym?" said Torquil. "*Gentlemen Only Ladies Forbidden.*" Gales of sycophantic laughter. Torquil continued: "Did you know that the word for sexual intercourse is not Anglo-Saxon but, back in the day, an eighteenth century legal acronym: *File Under Carnal Knowledge?*" The assembled throng paused for a moment then snorted a collective gaffaw.

Every utterance was making Travis fume and he dowsed his ire with lager. As he brooded he started saying the name over and over again in his head. 'Torquil Farquar' – what a stupid name. "Total Fucker more like."

The room went silent: did he just say that out loud? Perhaps six pints should be his limit, particularly given his current travails. Travis surveyed the

THE CHALLENGE

room surreptitiously over the top of his glass. The gang in the corner were all looking at him as if he had announced his intention to use the floor as a toilet. The TF in question had a face like a smacked arse. Travis could feel himself being scrutinised: his pony tail, big glasses, three-day beard, unwashed jeans and X-Men t-shirt – whatever test he was being put through he knew he had failed.

"Well, on that point compadres, I've got to go and shake hands with the wife's best friend," announced Torquil, turning to the door to the *Gents* directly behind him. His crew all stared at Travis. Some shook their heads and turned away while others gave him the evil eye. Travis ignored them and started to fish in his pocket for some loose change to get some Pork Scratchings. 'Compadres,' thought Travis. He couldn't work out if it was the affected American slang or the juvenile public school expressions that angered him most.

By the time Travis had decided that six pints was simply not enough and was ordering his seventh, Torquil came back, ready to pick up where he had left off. "Now, homeboys, where was I before someone had a senior moment and forgot his manners?" His 'homeboys' all sniggered and smirked at Travis.

That was it. Travis had had enough. What would Spider-man do? Obviously spray the TF in a microfine synthetic mesh, hang him from a street lamp and get a photograph in the *Fife Herald*, but that was out of the question. However, Travis was not going to let this one lie.

"Okay, Peter bloody Allis. If you know so much, care to back yourself? Fifty quid says I can beat you on any course – my choice." Travis stood arms akimbo in his best Superman pose. All that was missing was the fluttering cape and his underpants outside his jeans. For the first time in weeks he felt good and in control, despite all the evidence to the contrary.

Torquil looked at him as if he'd been slapped for a second time. Gathering his composure he said, "Fine, but care to make it interesting? Say ... five hundred?"

"If you're trying to get out of the challenge, fine, but it's fifty quid or nothing."

"Name the place and time," Torquil said affably.

Travis paused. The beer had most definitely clouded his judgement. "Ahh, let's see ... "

Travis's only real experience of golf was his Tiger Woods PS2 game and he realised that he had just jumped into a very deep hole of his own digging. Sweat started to break out across his forehead. His eyes met Torquil's even gaze. "Tarvit Hill," he blurted out. He had just managed to pull that out of the recesses of his memory – remembered from some National Trust leaflet he had picked up in his lawyer's office – but at least the bemused look on Torquil's face gave him a slight sense of relief.

"Sorry old chum, not familiar with Tarvit Hill golf club." One or two of the cronies smiled at the choice and one even nodded and winked at Travis, assuming it was a joke. "Behind the town on the road to Leven. It's on the map. See you on Sunday: be there or be square ... dude." He turned and went back to his table where his Blackberry was buzzing angrily with bad news.

Travis stood thinking fretfully as the early morning sun shone down on the estate, bathing Tarvit House's soft brown stone in the last traces of the copper-coloured dawn. What was he doing here? Why couldn't he just have said Augusta National and taken the Wii round to the TF's? What the hell was he thinking? What was he drinking more like.

Travis strode towards the small, slate-roofed building that acted as clubhouse, starter's hut and Pro shop. All that he knew about Tarvit House was that it was built at the start of the twentieth century by a Fredrick Sharp, as a home for his impressive art collection. The Sharps, like so many other families in the area at that time, had made their money in jute. In fact, they had even sold jute for sandbags to both sides in the American Civil War. Very sharp! Bloody home from home for Farquar, thought Travis.

Travis stood, waiting. For a moment he thought he heard RAF jets returning to Leuchars in the distance, until he realised that it was the TF pulling up in the car park in his custard-coloured Tesstarossa. He hadn't forgotten then. Minutes later the corpulent frame of Torquil Farquar could be seen ambling towards him, a vision in pastel, wearing a hotch-potch of reds, greens, purples and blues that, to Travis's mind, made him look like a walking packet of fruit gums. The ensemble was topped off with a flat cap worn back to front: of course. He carried a large golf bag, seemingly stuffed with golfing paraphernalia, but which could have comfortably housed a family of five.

"You won't be needing that," Travis said.

"Why not? Surrendering already?"

THE CHALLENGE

"Follow me," said Travis, and with a sideways jerk of the head he went into the starter's hut.

Torquil's white patent-leather golf shoes crunched on the floor as he inspected the treasure trove of golfing history that met his eyes. "The National Trust has recreated Sharp's original golf course and you have to play it with the original equipment," Travis stated matter-of-factly, as he idly picked up a thin canvas tube with a motley collection of clubs in it.

"Hickory shafts," said Torquil admiringly, as he lovingly stroked an old wooden driver. "Haskells," he went on.

"I beg your pardon?" said Travis.

"Conrad Haskell was a Cleveland dentist who invented the modern golf ball. These are reproduction Haskells," Torquil responded, holding one up to the light as if savouring a fine Chablis.

The two men strode on to the first tee. Correction: Torquil strode. Travis shambled reluctantly behind him.

"Generous fairways, not too much rough, no trees, no real bunkers and well-positioned flags on forgiving greens: what a pleasant way to earn fifty nicker." With that, Torquil teed up his ball, took out the driver and set himself: a quick wiggle of his toes, a waggle of the hips, a twitch at the wrist, then straight into his backswing and – whack. The ball fired off down the fairway and Torquil stood there admiring his handiwork. Travis's heart sank. The one thing he'd been hoping for was that Torquil was going to turn out to be all mouth and trousers, but sadly it was not to be.

"Care to step up to the plate, old love?" said Torquil slyly.

"So, what sort of thing did you do on weekends when you lived in the US?" Travis asked, more interested in the answer than in playing his shot.

Torquil eyed him up. "A couple of CEOs and I would take a Gulfstream down to Pebble Beach and play eighteen holes on Spyglass Hill, then fly back to the Hamptons in time for Sunday brunch. What do you do on a Sunday?"

"Check a few blogs, read emails, restart all my client servers and do some online maintenance," said Travis, as he rummaged in the bag for a club and a ball.

"Ah, you're in IT. How could I have missed the clues?" said Torquil sarcastically.

"Yes, that's the day job, but really I'm more Alan Moore than Gordon

Moore," Travis said proudly and puffed out his chest. Torquil looked confused.

"I write graphic novels in my spare time. My latest is set … "

"Woah there, cowboy. I've given up my Sunday to play golf with a man whose two loves are computers and comics. Holy crap!"

"So, what earth-shattering occupation did you do in America?" asked Travis, huffily.

"I ran a company specialising in derivatives," Torquil said, watching a couple of sparrows hunting for food on the ninth fairway.

"A shadow banker!" said Travis, stunned. What would Rorschach do if he got his hands on him? Hmm… Watchmen – not a good choice. He would probably join forces with the TF and force-feed Travis his mashy niblick. Travis's anger boiled up and he thrashed at the ball with his club. It spooned off the toe, hopped over the fence and landed thirty yards to his right.

"Hmm… The preferred lie is generally accepted to be the fairway, not the driveway, old chum."

Travis was as angry at the thought that his hero would side with Torquil as with his poor shot. "How do you think I feel spending my Sunday with one of the merchants that sold the world economy down the toilet?" Travis stomped off in search of his ball while Torquil sauntered off the tee towards his. At least one good thing about being a lousy golfer was that he would not have to spend too much time in Torquil's company!

By the third hole, Travis had decided to confront Torquil again. "You know I googled you. Very interesting. What was it that the little item on the Wall Street Journal website said? 'FBI investigation closes but British CEO forced to stand down by shareholders'?"

"Steady, old love, there is nothing illegal in what went down. Just a collection of talented and powerful individuals exercising their democratic right to make as much money as they could, which is the price you pay – "

"What price would that be? You've paid nothing – "

"If you'd let me finish … It's the price you pay to live in a democracy," said Torquil.

"While all these financial organisations were feathering their nests with this monetary jiggery pokery, they forgot that paying their dues was the price they paid to live in a democracy," snapped Travis.

"Get a grip. Nobody died," said Torquil.

THE CHALLENGE

"Yet," retorted Travis.

"I'm sorry – you must have mistaken me for someone who gives a toss. I would advise you not to push me, old boy. Cupar is a small place, you know."

Both men teed off in silence and stormed off in different directions to retrieve their balls. Travis had managed to find the one serious patch of rough on the course and started to hack away furiously, his oaths clearly audible across the fairway.

Torquil smiled and shouted over to him: "Did you know that that word is not actually Anglo-Saxon, but an eighteenth century legal acronym *File* ... ?"

"Oh, sod off!" Travis shouted back and finally hacked his ball out onto the fairway.

Hole five and the mood had simmered down. "So you did nothing wrong then?" said Travis, still pushing to get to the truth.

"Of course, purer than the driven proverbial," said Torquil, eyeing up his line to the flag.

"Pity. I had pictured you doing the perp walk and sharing a holding cell with a 400-pound walking tattoo from the Aryan brotherhood. Nasty!" smiled Travis.

Travis placed his ball and fired his usual drive off into the rough.

"You know, some people describe golf as a good walk ruined, but that shot is just taking the piss."

Travis mumbled darkly under his breath and shambled off in search of his ball.

Hole seven and, even though he had already lost his £50, Travis had become much more chipper. He had been baiting Torquil over the last two holes and TF was now losing his bonhomie.

"So Manhattan prices too rich for you? I mean, you may be innocent, but those fines for breaking the New York Stock Exchange rules, how much was it?"

"You seem to be getting particularly animated about all this," snapped Torquil.

"Funny that, when you can see fifteen years' worth of pension contributions evaporating before your very eyes."

"Talk to the hand, old chum, because this face ain't listening," huffed Torquil. There it was, that American slang again. It made Travis mad and he could feel himself having a Hulk moment – as if his skin was turning green and he was growing to five times his size. He lashed at his ball and – to his surprise – it arced off the tee some hundred yards away. Unfortunately it was still 60 degrees off true and he was back in the rough.

"So, how's the divorce going?" said Torquil in a mild and gentle tone

Travis scowled: "How did you know about that?"

Torquil smiled: "Cupar is a small town. Did I tell you my wife is a divorce lawyer? Had to use her maiden name because of the little shindig in NYC, but you should see her strut her stuff in court. Quite the little rottweiller … Good luck with that."

"Isn't that a breach of client confidentiality?" said Travis. His mind was already replaying all the grimmest moments in the breakdown of his marriage, the high decibel accusations and recriminations, the miserable days and lonely nights. What did the TF know and who told him?

"Let's drop it," he said, already beginning to sweat.

"I don't need my wife to tell tales out of school. Cupar is Gossip Central. You seem so keen to interrogate me for my missing moral fibre. What was it, domestic violence? Did she beat you?"

"Yes, fine. Now can I play this shot?"

"I don't know. You tell me," laughed Torquil.

Travis stared into the eyes of his nemesis. "What would you know about it?"

"Let me tell you, old son, I may be the devil's spawn whose soul is mortgaged to Mammon, but I didn't get here by not making absolutely sure I didn't have my opponent by the Haskells from the get go."

Travis looked at him: "What?"

"What a prick! And believe me, I'm in the prick business, so I know whereof I speak."

Travis was sweating profusely now. "Okay," he said trembling, "being in IT security has taught me a thing or two. What was it the FBI said about you?"

"You hacked the FBI computers? I don't believe it," Torquil countered scornfully.

"No, I hacked the email of the New York Times journalist who was following your case and he had some tasty quotes from them about you … You're right, you do know whereof you speak."

THE CHALLENGE

The two men stood staring at one another: who was going to blink first? Travis smiled nervously and reached for his club. The eighth hole was played in silence except for the gentle tweet of birdsong, the occasional passing car, the swish and whack of club on ball.

Travis was panicked by one thought: had he gone too far? Perhaps Torquil was now mad enough and might just decide to take the challenge to the next level. The perspiration poured out of Travis. Torquil stared at him angrily as the two walked on to the final tee.

Travis could hear the whoosh behind him as the TF swung a club angrily. Dark oaths followed as he marched up to take his shot.

When it was Travis's turn, he couldn't stop the sweat running into his eyes. He took a swing at the ball, missed and the impetus on the follow through made the club shoot from his sweaty grasp.

"What the – " said a startled Torquil as the club caught him a glancing blow on the side of the head. He staggered back over his golf bag and fell off the tee in a graceless heap.

"File under carnal knowledge?" asked Travis. He waddled over to help Torquil to his feet.

"My bad! I deserve that. Too many hours being interrogated by FBI forensic accountants. Talking shop gets me on the defensive."

"If that was you being defensive, I'd hate to catch you when you were being offensive."

The two men putted out on the ninth and went to turn in their clubs. Travis wandered back to his car and then turned to face Torquil: "Look, as days go, this is probably one that I would care to forget, but actually I think something good might come of it."

"You're giving up golf?"

"I'm going to call Carol and try to mend some fences."

The two men looked at one another, then Travis turned and unlocked his car.

"Oh, there is one more thing," said Torquil

"Yes?"

"You still owe me fifty quid."

VANTAGE POINT

Faye Stevenson

The last of the sun's rays penetrated the windscreen. "Sitting here, you'd be forgiven if you thought it was summer," yawned Bob – a yawn that said I am so comfortable I could fall asleep.

The view from the car park, halfway up Falkland Hill, was impressive: an intricate patchwork of pastel greens, browns and pale yellows spread out beneath them, trimmed with a satin blue sea.

"It's bloody cold so you'll need to wrap up," Janice snapped.

Bob sighed and left her to pack up what remained of their picnic while he relieved himself at the front of the car. Their Fiesta was tucked into the farthest corner of the parking area to ensure that he would have some privacy should he need it. He had become an expert at finding discreet places. He tried not to take his water tablets before a longish journey especially if there was no guarantee of toilet facilities en route, or at their destination.

Bob straightened up, stretched his long neck as if he were about to crow, and gazed south-east out over the Forth. The Bass Rock, the tall tower of Cockenzie Power Station and Edinburgh's Arthur's Seat, gave some indication of where the capital and the seaside resorts of East Lothian were located on the coastline opposite.

It was Christmas Eve and they were spending the night in Strathmiglo with their daughter Shona, her partner and little Cara, Bob and Janice's only grandchild. Before his triple by-pass, Bob had been a keen hiker. Nowadays, he was frightened to climb the stairs to his bedroom. He knew this annoyed Janice, especially when the rehabilitation clinic had assured them he was more able than he thought. He still gave his walking boots an airing but tended to avoid anything too strenuous. That's why he liked Falkland Hill car park – it was flat! And he could look over towards Perth and see Schiehallion, one of his first Munros.

A familiar tinkling of "Pink! Pink! Pink! Pink!" caused him to look upwards.

VANTAGE POINT

A skene of Pink-footed geese flew overhead. He shielded his eyes from the sun and watched a long V-shaped streak across the sky. They looked like two straggly, black laces flapping in the wind, sometimes forming a perfect V, then wavering every few seconds before straightening up again.

"See them: they'll have been feasting at our Shona's. There's a big tattie field on the left-hand side just before you get into Strath," Bob explained. "They're making their way back to Loch Leven for the night."

Janice shrugged and said nothing. Bob watched her as she struggled to pull a jaded fleece down over her body. He slipped with ease into his winter waterproofs.

"I can't wait til New Year's over so that I can get back to normal, eat normal food again," Janice wheezed. She rubbed her face, stretching the skin tight around her eyes. Her middle fingers massaged her temples. She looked worn out.

He tried cajoling her. "Forget about your diet for the time being. It's Christmas. Anyway, I like you just the way you are."

"Oh, you would!"

Bob couldn't fathom women. Janice's size had never bothered him. They watched as other couples and young families returned from their outing. Janice swung round.

"You know, Bob, I could do with a walk up the hill. I'd like more of a challenge than skulking around here like a bloody geriatric." She paused then added, "Are you coming or do I go myself?"

"Jan, if I could … It's too … difficult … I'm no' able."

"For goodness sake, listen to yourself. You're not the Bob Shand I knew. I'm only asking you try a wee walk. We can take our time."

How many thoughts can bombard a human mind in ten seconds? Bob felt weighted by his: indecisions, insecurities.

"Well?"

"Let's go for it." He hoped he sounded more enthusiastic than he felt. Janice had been uncharacteristically tetchy lately and he was keen to ensure that the next two days passed without a hitch. He rummaged the boot for his binoculars, taking care not to tip over a large Tupperware of gravy Janice had warned him about. The boot was jam-packed with overnight bags, Christmas presents and too much food. A cooked turkey embalmed in tin foil had been wedged into the back. Everything smelled of sage-and-onion stuffing. It lingered as it does after the fridge door has been closed. They set off arm in arm, Bob decked out as if he were about to attempt Mount Everest, Janice as if she had just popped out to the local shops – in a hurry. The afternoon car park was emptying quickly.

"Watch you don't slip. There's still a lot of frost lying," he warned.

Janice looked down at her shabby trainers and said, "Shona borrowed my brogues. She needed a sturdy pair of shoes for work."

The beginning of the trek was muddy so they opted to walk amongst the heather. The vegetation became more sparse the further up they climbed. Gorse bushes and brown heather gave way to silvery, pale grass. It should have been about ankle deep, except the strong westerly winds had transformed it into a shag-pile carpet that had been hoovered in the same direction. Winter's cold hand numbed their faces and its icy breath burned the back of their throats. Bob began to revel in the familiarity. Janice pulled the collar of her fleece over her chin and ears – only her red nose and curly, white hair were visible. It looked as if a small cloud had settled on her shoulders.

The East Lomond, or Falkland Hill as it was known locally, had been Bob's playground. His summers had been spent either playing cricket or roaming between East and West Lomond with his friends. They'd poke at animal droppings with sticks to establish what had been eaten, or spy on grouse scurrying incessantly amongst the heather. Bob's keen eye could track a skylark as it landed some thirty metres from its chicks. Then, to confuse a sparrow hawk, should one be hovering above, the bird would zigzag across the mottled terrain to where its young were nesting.

Now it was two aeroplanes, side by side, high in the sky that had caught Janice's attention. Falkland Hill was directly beneath the flight path from Europe to North America. A white, powdery line trailed behind them. They were like two speed boats racing across a calm, tropical sea.

"Lucky them," she sighed.

Bob looked up. "That'll be us again one day," he promised.

Janice took a handkerchief from her pocket and walked away from him. The wind speed had picked up considerably. As she glanced back over her shoulder, she called out something. Bob screwed his face and held his hand to his ear to indicate he hadn't heard her words; they'd been swallowed by the

VANTAGE POINT

galloping wind and were blustering eastwards towards the Neuk of Fife. Janice simply turned on her heel and stormed off.

Bob was bewildered. Wasn't she the one who wanted the walk in the first place? He urged Janice to slow down, as he searched tentatively for a safe footing. The ground beneath them was hard and would provide no cushion should either of them slip on the black trickles of water that had turned to ice on the grey rocks and permeated the coarse short grass.

As he struggled to close the gap, he could see that Janice had stopped at the lower boundary. A couple were showing a small child how to open and close a gate in the wooden fencing. Safely through, the young family were now heading in Bob's direction when suddenly the woman raced back towards his wife. The two of them exchanged a few words. The pretty blonde smiled and mouthed 'Merry Christmas' to Bob as she passed him to rejoin the others in her group. The short interlude had given Bob a chance to catch up.

"What was that about?" he asked.

"She'd dropped her car keys. I saw them as I was shutting the gate. She was lucky," Janice mimicked a posh accent, "she'd left the spare set in Edinburgh."

"She seemed nice enough."

"Did she?" remarked Janice, "Took her all her time to say thank you."

Janice resumed her pace but Bob paused to take in what remained of the day. He knew that, down in the village, street lamps would be competing with Christmas tree lights and the huge flood-lights illuminating the twelfth-century walls of Falkland Palace. However, out in the open, the sky held the light just a little longer and the onset of darkness could catch you unawares.

At the bottom, only two cars remained – their Fiesta and a Land Rover Discovery that was parked near the entrance. Bob scanned the area for Janice and assumed she was festering in the car. The sound of something heaving with exertion startled him and unnerved him in the eerie silence that followed. He swivelled 360 degrees but couldn't pinpoint where it was coming from. He waited. A frightening crash of shattering glass caused him to dash towards the black Land Rover. Immediately he thought of his wife.

"Janice!" he screamed. "Stay in the car!" Then he stopped, and stared incredulously.

Janice had folded down one of the back seats of the Discovery. She had squeezed her upper body into the tight space between the seat and the back and began tossing handfuls of Christmas presents and wrapping paper on to the half-frozen mud behind her. A large stone supported her weight.

"Janice! Stop it!" Bob demanded.

She took no notice. Desperately, he reached in, grabbed hold of her clothing with his right hand and took a firm grip of her hair with his left and heaved her out. She bounced off the door and they staggered backwards, scattering paper and gifts in their way. Bob held Janice in a body lock. Despite her struggling and protestations, he knew that he couldn't let go. They birled and whirled for what seemed like an eternity but were, in fact, a few frenzied moments. Undeterred, the wind sneaked in and snatched some brightly coloured wrapping paper from beneath their feet.

"Jan! You're gonna kill me!"

Janice let out a low moan that grew louder and deeper with each laboured breath. Bob held on. Eventually, he felt her body go limp – like a child's does when sleep takes over.

"What were you thinking?" he beseeched.

Janice held her face in her hands. The space between her fingers revealed her eyes were closed. "I was jealous. They had a car full of presents that they didn't need. They were happy, she was pretty – and slim. All lah-deh-dah. And a man that cared."

"I care!" he protested.

"Not us. Them - Shona and that bloody, lazy man o' hers." She leaned against Bob for support. "I wanted wee Cara to wake up tomorrow and have everything she's asked for." She surveyed the chaos. "God, what have I done?"

Part of him was furious at her and wanted to give her a good shake but he'd seen the fear in her eyes. She gathered up a large doll and what looked like a child's carrying case. In her haste, boxes began to topple from her arms as she leaned down to pick up more. In despair, she dropped them all - except one. With the cuff of her fleece, she wiped some mud from the doll's cheek then held it to her chest and began to cry.

"Help me, Bob! Pleee-ase!" she wailed.

For the first time in a long time, Bob looked at Janice, really looked at her. This was his wife, who had supported him throughout his illness, who had visited him as often as she could, who couldn't drive and had taken the bus – on a four-hour round trip. Who had just been there. Unfailing. He'd been so

VANTAGE POINT

taken up with his own troubles that he'd never considered what it must have been like for her.

"C'mon, Janice," he said gently, as he led her, still weeping, back to the car. She was shivering – with cold or shock or both, he concluded.

Once he had warmed Janice, he would put all the parcels back. Alone, he would think of a resolution. The engine gave three feeble wheezy coughs then – nothing. Bob pumped the accelerator. Push, push, push. He twisted the ignition key. His body bounced in rhythm to the silent chugging as he willed it to kick in.

"What's happening?"

Her unanswered question throbbed in his head as he pounded the ground outside. Think, think, think!

A white Nissan Micra careered into the car park, narrowly missing Bob. A group of youths jeered as the small Micra screeched into reverse and jetted backwards, as if the rewind button had been thumped. The boom-booming of the music reverberated around him before being sucked into the emptiness as the car and its occupants dipped into the depths of the hillside.

Bob opened the door and knelt down beside Janice.

"They'll be here any minute. We have to get our story straight," he insisted softly.

Calmly he devised a tale that would, hopefully, satisfy the owners of the Discovery. He'd blame young lads in a light-coloured motor - one that had been parked further down the slope. Bob and Janice were finishing off a coffee when they heard a commotion. On seeing Bob, they ran off. Unfortunately, neither of them got a good look at the youths or the car.

As Bob watched the young family negotiate the last part of their descent, the darkening sky stalked them silently.

"Your car has been broken in to," he blurted as they approached. "Sorry."

Glossy Christmas wrapping paper lay crumpled and torn amidst a large pile of presents. A few small ones remained intact and some had their corners ripped back revealing the surprise inside. There was a gaping black hole in the side window of the Land Rover. The jagged edges sparkled and reflected the moonlight behind the observers. Night had descended rapidly.

"What happened?" barked the young man as he reached into the glove compartment and retrieved a large torch.

Under the interrogation of the torchlight, Bob stuck to his story although he did feel guilty as he watched the young mother struggle to shield her two small children from the toys and clothing scattered on the frosty surface.

"Didn't you chase after them?"

"My husband has a heart condition," Janice called out feebly from the shadows, then she slumped on a low bench behind the Discovery.

Bob would have preferred if she had remained in the car. However, he gestured towards her saying, "This whole thing gave my wife a terrible fright."

"I'm so sorry," apologised the young man, "that was stupid of me."

"I can give you my name and address if you like – for the insurance," Bob offered.

He wondered how he would have reacted to the family's predicament if Janice had not been the perpetrator. Would he have shown more compassion? Been angrier? He was relieved when the young couple said they didn't want it to affect their no claims bonus and equally relieved when they agreed that calling the police would be a waste of everyone's time. Darkness and Christmas Eve were an unfortunate combination (though fortunate for us, Bob couldn't help thinking).

"You were in the car when you heard the crash?" the young man persisted as he checked the back seat for fragments of glass.

Bob held the torch. "We were in the car but we didn't hear anything, except the wind. We saw some boys hovering suspiciously. I thought, if I get out, they would move on."

Bob, all six foot two of him, had a physique that belied his recent ill health. His military training was evident. He strode as if several wooden coat hangars were strapped to his back. Most people would think twice about having a go.

"I can't understand it. Why would they think that we had presents in the car? Why not go for the Sat Nav? Or my CDs. Why didn't the alarm go off?"

Bob, genuinely, couldn't explain the last one either.

"I'll bring our car over. It'll give you some light," he insisted. He'd probably flooded the engine with his last attempt but he prayed that this time it would start. Miraculously, it did.

Janice tried to help distract the children who had been plonked in the front while the glass was being cleared from the back seat. Bob passed their belongings to the young father who piled everything back into the car – with

VANTAGE POINT

a little more care than when they had been cast out. To every "Is that a ... ?" from the youngsters, a sharp "No!" sprang from their mother's lips.

Once the car had been reorganised and the back area had been checked thoroughly for anything sharp, the children were strapped into their seats. They exchanged polite thank yous and Merry Christmases. In his rear view window Bob saw the young couple, ethereal-like, engulfed in exhaust fumes, as the Fiesta juddered its way down the hill.

"Do you think they believed us?" Janice asked with her puffy eyes fixed on the blackness behind them.

"I think they had their doubts, but knew they'd have a hard job proving it. How did you know there were presents in the back?"

"She told me when I handed over the keys." Janice lowered her eyes. "The irony is – the car door was open all the time. If I'd tried it first, instead of smashing the window with that bloody stupid boulder ... " She shook her head. "Please don't say anything ... to anyone, especially Shona. I don't know what came over me."

Bob squeezed his wife's hand gently.

"I think I do," he said, "I think I do."

LOCATION – PERTHSHIRE

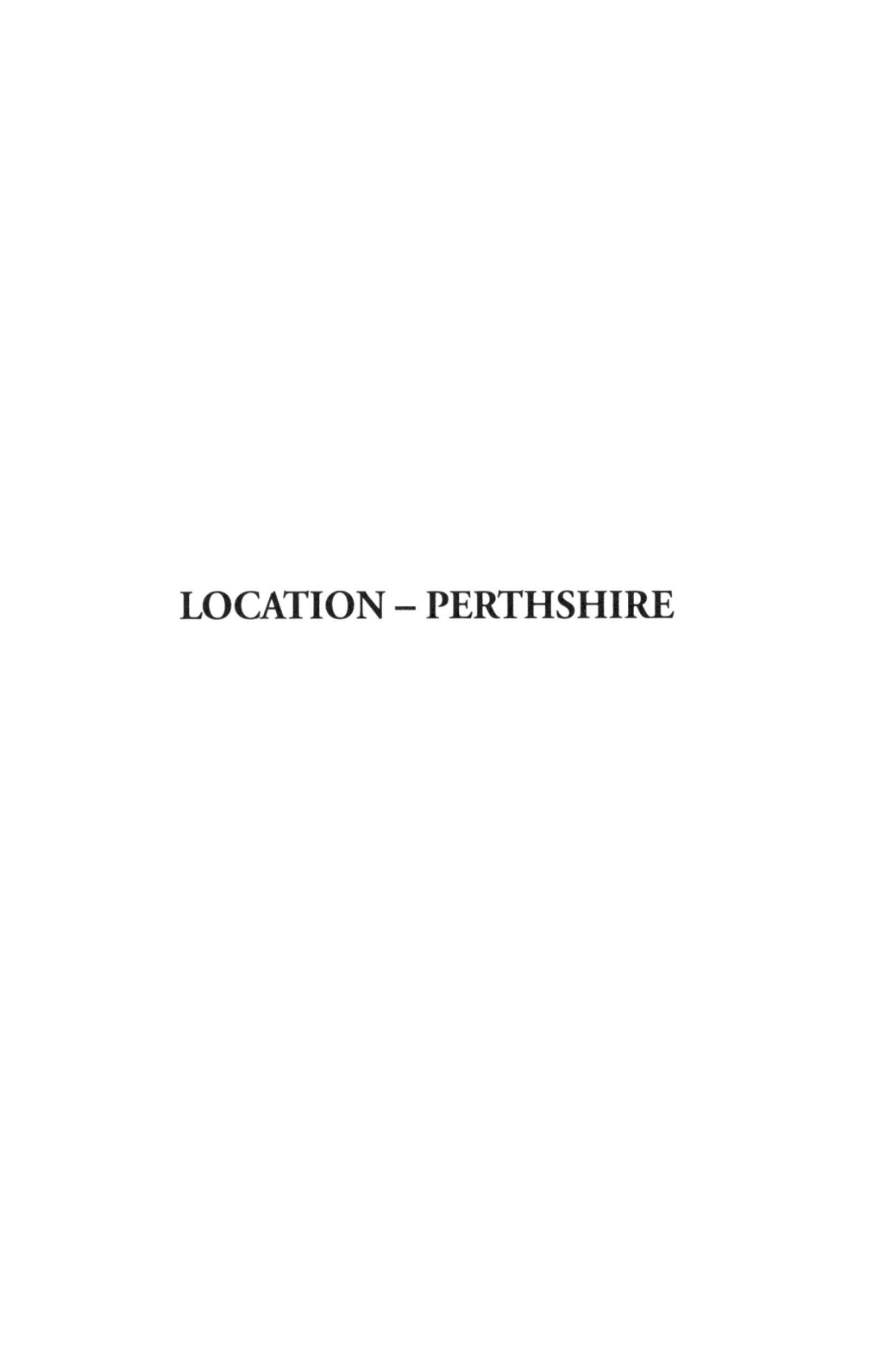

SINDERIN

Roddie McKenzie

The track from Kinnaird to the top of the brae was steep; it was already warm in the morning sun. From under my hat the sweat trickled down my forehead. I paused to sweep the salty sting from my eye and to allow my horse to regain his chuffing breath. I felt a weariness dragging at my limbs and a boulder weighing down my hammering heart. Yet it had nothing to do with our trot up that long uphill track, rutted with wheel tracks. I was just the factor's clerk – why could Airlie not come out himself to do his own dirty work? But then, he had given me his word …

Below, blue-green hedges outlined the buff and ochre rhombuses of fields that stretched out towards the Tay. The river widened east, merging into the pale golden sky, crowned by the globe of the recently risen sun. As I rounded the shoulder of Guardswell Hill, I saw the twin summits of Balgay Hill and The Law rise from the prostrate body of the Carse. Looking right, across the river, the sienna and umber scumbled hills of Fife rose to the twin peaked plateau of The Lomonds: the "Paps of Fife". Ahead the village nestled like a sleeping babe in a hollow under the slopes of Pitmiddle Hill.

The track bent to the right, passing through a gate in a dry stone dyke flanked by a windbreak of ash trees. A barely audible swish drew my attention to their gently waving branches, as if, ironically, they were welcoming me to the settlement. As I clattered over the burn on the wooden bridge, I glimpsed a wraith of smoke rising from the treed slopes of Pitmiddle and heard the cry of disturbed grouse. The breeze brought an acrid whiff of usquebaugh and I smiled: that dodger Jamie Baxter was still up to his old tricks. For three years I had turned a blind eye to his shenanigans. After all, live and let live.

At the two cross lanes the cottages stood, rough built of drystone and thatched with heather. Their gable ends faced the main street, casting languid shadows across the lanes in the early light of this warm March morn, in the year of our Lord, 1851. I dismounted and tied Bucephalus's reins to the base

SINDERIN

of a currant bush.

Last season had been a good year for the fruit, and if this gentle Spring held, the women would make a good return from the tangled horns of gooseberry and shrubbery of currant bushes that occupied the strip of gardens by the cottage doors. My foot caught in a fresh hoofprint in the earthen roadway softened by, and still glistening with dew. As I stumbled I caught a glimpse of my face reflected in a cottage window. I had seen cheerier faces on the condemned being driven away in the black Marias from the Dundee High Court.

The cows had not long been driven by the lad to graze on Pitmiddle Hill. I realised this as I looked down, cursed and extracted my foot from a steaming cow pat. As I did I noticed a torn and hoof-printed sheet of paper. The familiar copperplate script drew my attention and I stooped to pick it up and dusted it off against my plus-fours. I thought so. It was Archibald McKinlay`s hand-drawn sketch for the fencing off of Outfield and Guardswell. I was too late. The news was out.

No one in the village had yet stirred nor had anyone appeared at the wells at either end of the street. A creaking door behind drew my eye to the gardens behind the cottages; no, it was only someone going back indoors after throwing out meal for the hens that were nodding and clucking in their wire-fenced pen. From two of the chimneys thin grey clouds were already meandering and the smell of bonfire reminded me of a happier time last Guy Fawkes night on Magdalen Green with Elsie. It displaced the earthy smell of manure newly spread over the rigs on the Outfield.

"So ye are nae blate to show yer face here *Maister* McGilvary?"

My reverie broken, I turned to face the source of the rasping voice. Aye, it was Sandy Reid, my lass's father. A ruddy-faced man in his fifties, he blocked my path, his hands clenched in front gripping a horn-handled walking stick of bumped blackthorn. The breeze flicked grey locks of hair against the sides of his stained flat cap.

"Sandy, I beg your pardon, for that is why I am here n-n-now to tell you and your neighbours of the Laird's new arrangements for leasing the pastures. I don't know what Archibald …"

"Aye maybe so," he snapped. "But at least he was man enough to tell us and no tae come skulking in after the fact. Just when were you – oor supposed mid man – going to tell us that Allan of Errol was taking away maist of our land?"

My throat was dry, my voice croaked. "Sandy please, don't turn your back on me. Please let me come into the house. It needn't be as bad as you think."

"No Davie. Ye'll be welcome intae ma hoose nae mair - neither by me nor by Elsie. Good day to ye, sir!"

He slammed his door so hard that the currant canes danced. Heads began to appear around open doorways. I sighed heavily and fumbled in my pocket for the Laird's proclamation as the curious crowd assembled.

I read the proclamation, aware of the quiver in my voice. "On this twenty third of March, eighteen hundred-and-fifty one ..."

The details of the fencing operation were explained. Looking up from the parchment, I saw their faces first blank with shock, then taut with anger. Fists were waved and I felt the sweat on my spine as the circle narrowed. I heard their angry muttering around me like the howling of a feral pack.

Hamish's voice boomed over the clamour. "So the Laird wants to fence off Outfield? Where are we to graze our beasts? This enclosure will tak away the best pasture land."

I coughed and fingered the proclamation. "Hamish, his lordship needs to ensure that the estate pays its way. By renting Outfield he will increase his rental income from the estate and in the long term this will provide security for you all."

My words fell like ash into the breeze. They were not convinced, and neither was I.

"McKinlay's men will complete the fencing by the middle of the week. I am sorry there is nothing more I can say. Any cattle found inside the fence after Monday will be impounded on his Lordship's orders. My friends, these are hard times for laird and tenant alike – it is the only way forward and ... there is nothing more that I can do."

I heard the spittle splat onto the ground behind me as I edged through the crowd, unhitched Bucephalus, mounted and rode out and thundered over the bridge. Pausing briefly, I tacked the proclamation to a tree trunk by the bridle track. I deemed it too risky to fix it to the well-head as I had intended. Sandy's door remained shut as I glanced back before riding downhill to Kinnaird.

SINDERIN

I had completed my rounds of the Carse tenancies early on the Friday evening a week later. It had been sad work right enough, bringing notice of rent rises to folk barely scratching a living as it was from that heavy dank clay. I had repaired to the change house in Raitt village for a beer to slake my thirst from a long sweat-drenched day in the saddle, hoping to raise my sagging spirits before the journey back to my room in the factor's croft at Abernyte.

The inn was quiet, being early. Many were still a-field and the acrid fog of pipe smoke had yet to fill the room and the drystone jointing of the walls was still geometric. I was staring into the depths of the pewter tankard at the last suds of beer when the door clattered open. A chubby-faced man of stocky build stood in the doorway.

"Ach, Davie MacGillvary, ye look like a man thit hae lost a shilling and found a bawbee!"

"Jamie Baxter, ye don't seem to me to be a man that would be in need of the services of the change house – or maybe ye are here in some official capacity?"

"Just a traveller in need of rest, like yersel." He came up to my table. "And perhaps ye could be a wee bit more discreet, Maister Davie," he whispered.

"Will ye have a beer, Jamie?" I placed my purse on the table.

"Aye, well, I have a drouth right enough. That is very kind of you, Maister Davie."

As the landlord walked back to the bar, Jamie reached for his tankard. I barely let him take a mouthful before I launched into my question.

"How are things in Pitmiddle?"

Jamie paused and wiped the froth from his greying beard. "Folks are angry, aye, but resigned. They realise that there is nothing they can do. The Laird's word is law."

I shifted uneasily in my seat. Jamie noticed and continued.

"Ye mustna blame yerself, Maister Davie. The villagers dinna. We all ken it was a job ye didna want."

I sighed heavily. "It is kind of ye to say so, Jamie. This duty has been hard on me. It has driven a wedge between myself and Elsie."

"Aye, aye … Hard it must be for you, for Sandy is a stubborn beast. All the more pity, for she obeys his every word."

"It is true what you say?"

"Aye."

"Jamie, could you do me a great favour? Could you get a message to her?" My quill and paper were already out of my saddle bag.

Two days later I was waiting for her, my cloak wrapped against the cold south-westerly wind. Bucephalus was grazing in the shelter of Pitmiddle wood above the village. I took out my pocket watch. It was past noon. She was ten minutes late.

For reassurance I turned and looked over at Jamie Hay's deserted croft on the brae above the village. The sun kissed the rough stone walls and flecks of mica glistened like dewdrops. Many times I had been drawn up that beckoning path to gaze over the Carse. In my mind's eye, I could see Elsie on the doorstep, the weans at her feet. With the conifer bowing to me in the wind and that pungent scent of rosemary tumbling down the path like an unrolling carpet, I could feel that comfortable sense of home wrapping around me like a soft, warm blanket as I walked, weary from my day's toil, over my own yard, over my own land, to my own door. This place we could restore, when I got the lease. Airlie had said so. Or was that my thirty pieces of silver?

Then I caught that glimpse of gold, the reflected sunlight on her wheat-coloured hair and her elfin face as she pushed aside the shadows and brambles on the path side with her shawl.

"Elsie, my darling, it is grand tae see you. Sit down and let us work this out."

She hung back and I had a sense of foreboding.

"Davie, I cannae stay long, Faither thinks that I am at Widow Mauchline's."

"How is it with Sandy? Has he come round any?"

"No Davie," her voice was breaking. "He thinks that this will destroy the village in time."

"Darling, I know that this is not the best of things, but Airlie has promised me the cottage. We would have what we have dreamed of – our own home. We could be wed by Candlemas. I could spend the rest of the summer getting the house ready."

"Davie." Her eyes moistened and glistened as her voice cracked. "My

SINDERIN

faither has always thought ye an honourable man, a good man, but he cannae thole this. Folk will lose their livelihood. He says there are no enough young folk leaving for prospects in the Carse. This enclosure will strangle farming here."

"Elsie, but *we* will not be farmers! You can mind the berries around the croft for the jam man, but we will have my wage - and maybe when Airlie is too fat to sit a horse, I'll be the factor."

She sniffed and turned away. I ran to her. She was enclosed by my arms, but her litheness was gone. Stiff, like lumber, she was propped against me.

"Davie, ye'll be a factor of nothing. Faither says, wi the farming gone the village will die."

"But the Laird says that this enclosure is needed for progress, otherwise the estate will wither."

"Aye, maybe. Lairds mun dae whit lairds dae but Faither was telt by McKinlay that the enforcement was a job that Airlie was sly enough to pass on and ye were not hard persuaded to take it on." She wiped her eyes as a tone of despair buckled her voice.

"Wid ye really tak ma cousin's beasts when they let them graze the Outfield? That's what it wid mean, Davie."

"My lass, I done it for us, for our future."

"We have no future now. Can you no see that? He will never forgive you now, nor would the village. We would be shunned! *You* have killed our future." The tears flowed. "And all this time I dreamt of the day when you would free me from him."

She gathered her skirts and ran down the path, heedless of the thorns. I thought to follow but was rooted, pole-axed by her last remark. Damn Airlie! He said it would be an exercise of my initiative. She was out of my sight when I heard her heart-wrung sobbing.

As I came down the hill, towards Abernyte, I glanced ruefully over my shoulder. The village seemed entrenched behind that stockade of ash trees. As the sun arced to the South, shadows filed like sentries into the thickets behind the dyke and behind the gate. It was no use. That way was barred and lost to me now. Damn Airlie! He said it would be an exercise of my initiative.

I remember less of the following months, the days passing like so many petals dropping off the passing summer blooms, the letters that I wrote to her and the replies that never came. My days passed in a daze, mainly in the depths of Pitmiddle wood with Jamie Baxter. Soon the croft, horse and job passed like so much smoke from the still, out through the trees and away, high over the Carse. The best laid plans o' mice and men ... I never went back to Pitmiddle. Yet whenever I met any of the villagers in my stupor, I remembered no bitterness or hatred. All passion was spent. Instead there was nothing but pity in their shocked, staring eyes.

Then in late August I had had enough.

The *Balaena* twisted at anchor in the morning swell. We were waiting in mid- channel to clear the stowaways and for the *Polar Star* to clear the Victoria Dock. Then we were underway for the Arctic. My gear was stowed below in my berth. Jimmie Baxter's pal, Erchie Hay, had put in a good word for me and I was signed up for the eight month voyage. I leaned on the taffrail as the ship creaked.

The clump of sea-boots on the planked deck caused me to turn and see Erchie approach. Then his tattooed forearms leaned beside me on the polished rail. I was aware he was looking at me as I stared landward.

"Are you no coming below Davie? Eck has opened a braw cask."

"No, Erchie, I`ll stay here for now."

" Aye, aye ... Nae regrets then Davie?"

"No Erchie, no regrets. I`ll be glad to be away."

Down the Carse, I picked out the green cap of Pitmiddle wood above the village and stared into the far distance.

"Ye'll be thinking of home eh? A lang time before we see it again; a lot of lads find it hard on their first voyage, that last look at the hills of home."

"No, Erchie, the sense of that place is lost to me now."

"Whit? But ye will have friends and family ye will be leaving behind. Does that no bother ye?"

"No, Erchie, there was a place that was home to me once and a home that could have been, but when the people have gone what is a place but a space and a time that once you filled with memories? When the people have gone, the place is just an empty eggshell. There is nothing there for me any more and it's time to be moving on."

Erchie looked long at me, before drawing his gnarled hand over his brow. He flicked up his head and laughed aloud.

SINDERIN

"Ach, are you not the deep one indeed and me just a simple tar."

He turned and shook his head, laughing a laugh like the bark of sea lion as he clambered down the aft hatchway.

RELEASE – GLENFARG

Pat Fox

A silence came –
so sudden and so quickly gone
we could not recognise it –
thought it was a noise itself.

On the hilltop
there had been a saugh of wind,
a ripple and a running,
somewhere some water.
In the heather, we had heard
a scutter and a pounce,
forcing the stems apart.
We had heard whaups
and the aggression of bees.
Our ears had caught the rasp of leaves
against the birch-tree boles
– and from the glen-head had risen
the rip and tear of traffic
scratching the background air.

And then, for one nano-second,
there was no sound.

THE STONE OF THE SIDLAWS

David Carson

It was while walking with his dog that he came across the stone – nearly fell over it in fact.

The middle-aged man and his Westie were a regular sight in the hills. They looked at ease with each other, and although the man was not himself given to displays of emotion, he enjoyed the dog's gleeful barks when he said they were going into the "Seedlees."

The Sidlaws are modest in height and appearance. They don't go in for grandiose gestures – no knife-edged ridges and few steep cliffs. To the north, gentle slopes slide down to Strathmore, petering out to become fields of barley, wheat, potatoes and, in spring and summer, bright seas of daffodils and oil-seed rape; and although they cast the odd frown southwards in the direction of the Carse, they are nowhere intimidating.

In times gone by, drovers would take cattle from one side of the hills to the other, and remnants of these old roads still survive in shallow glens. Nowadays the roads that cross the hills break them into separate but related groups. The man liked to imagine them as a friendly extended family, welcoming without pretension the visitors who came to relax in their company. If drawn to fanciful reflection, he reckoned that he himself resembled these hills. He was a quiet, understated sort of chap who shied away from extremes and who, because he promised little, rarely disappointed.

On this particular Saturday afternoon, he was walking the stretch between the quarry at Collace and the Ballo hills above Tullybaccart, with Black Hill and the King's Seat the destination. He liked the extensive views from here. It's not true what they say about familiarity, he thought. Here it breeds only joy. His gaze took in the Tay estuary, and Dundee and beyond, the hills of Fife. The dog merely sniffed the ground.

"And look up there", he pointed, "that's Schiehallion, where you had all that fun with a dead rabbit." As if understanding the man's gesture, the dog nodded vigorously and barked.

Much of the ground they were on was covered in thick, high heather, which made progress difficult for a short-legged dog. Her solution was to develop a Zebedee-like propensity for springing rather than walking. Nevertheless she tended to disappear for moments at a time. It was while looking anxiously for her presumed whereabouts that he banged his shin against something rough and hard. The offending object was a stone, considerably overgrown by heather and grass. He pulled at the undergrowth to get a better look and saw at once that the stone was where it was by design and not by chance. A shallow trench, now hardly visible, had been dug in the earth to embed it firmly.

The stone itself was not large, about two feet high by a foot wide, and was oval in shape but straight at the base. Both sides were host to extensive patches of grey lichen, relieved by bright blotches of yellow moss. He knelt down. Almost absent-mindedly, he began to scrape at the lichen. It crumbled and fell to the ground, leaving behind a light-coloured pattern on the wrinkled surface of the stone. A bit like skin with the elastoplast peeled off, he thought. He looked round nervously, as if guilty that he might be caught interfering where he shouldn't.

Then he noticed what seemed like indentations. He cleaned off the lichen and moss more methodically, and soon he had uncovered a letter on one side of the stone – a B. There was something like a letter on the other side, but it was so worn and indistinct that he couldn't make it out. A boundary mark, he wondered, or some kind of memorial?

He looked down at the stone again, and stiffened slightly. It struck him that it was set at an angle that cut across the natural lie of the land. One side pointed in the direction of Dundee, the other to a break in the slope leading to the King's seat. He lay down and eyed the horizon. I thought so, he muttered. The dog, somewhat bemused by his antics, had started to bark.

"Shush, it's just a bit intriguing, that's all." The barks turned to whines, and the dog began to scratch the ground with increasing agitation. "Come on Kirstie," he said, "no need for that." He spoke more sharply than he had intended for he had become aware of a tingling in the hair at the back of his neck. "Let's get to the top of the King's Seat, then go home".

Home was a bothy, one of several outbuildings belonging to a farm that lay near Collace village. He had noticed it during one of his walks and had made enquiries. The bothy had had several tenancies in the past, but it was now available for purchase. He resolved, with a decisiveness that surprised him, to buy it.

Normally he enjoyed the walk up the lane and the sight of his house as he rounded the last bend – the gable end covered in red and green ivy, and the solitary rowan tree adjacent to the door. Today, however, he felt vaguely uneasy after his walk. He opened the door and squeezed past the bicycle he kept in the hallway. The dog made straight for her dish and slurped her water noisily. The man stared round the room and, unable to settle, went outside again. He studied the regular sides and the blunt top of Dunsinnan hill, still visible in the fading light. He thought he could see something glinting on the summit. The man blinked, and whatever it was disappeared. The grass in the fields opposite rustled like unfinished whispers, and his gaze swept over them and upwards to where they merged with the darkening lower slopes of the hills. It was only when he looked at the branches of the rowan, with their leaves hanging limp and motionless, that he realised there was not a breath of wind. He went back into his house and closed the door firmly behind him.

The following morning dawned bright and dry. The man had passed a restless night, but he reckoned that a day of positive activity would banish his unease. He had for some time been thinking of enlarging the bothy into a cottage. There was plenty of space to expand the building because the pendicle lay empty. Previous tenants had grown vegetables there, and it had even been home to a pig or a cow in days gone by. He had plans to build an extension and attach to it a lean-to, a sort of basic conservatory. In truth, however, his plans were evolving slowly, and the only evidence of progress was piles of slates and breeze blocks lying at the rear of the house.

After his bowl of porridge, he set about examining the wall that would in due course be one side of his planned extension. He walked round the outside of the house, pacing, measuring and testing how solid the wall was at various points. He moved indoors. The wall on this side was covered in plasterboard, and he decided he would have to remove some of it to assess the condition of the bricks and of the cement binding them together. He fetched a ladder and, having selected an area high up in the corner, he began to chip gently. A fine dirty-grey spray tumbled down the wall, followed by a solid chunk of plaster. The man smoothed away the ragged edges left behind, then muttered to himself in annoyance. He had gone too high and revealed not brick, but a section of wooden joist.

He was about to start again lower down when his eye was caught by some marks in the wood. At the same time he became aware of Kirstie looking up at him, and his uneasiness returned. "I'll need to get a proper look," he said, prising away some more of the plaster. Gradually he revealed a primitive-looking drawing consisting, he saw eventually, of three parts. The first was like a triangle with the top removed, perhaps the outline of a flat-topped hill; the second was a figure of what looked like a man, matchstick style; and the third was the letter B.

The man stared at the drawing. He was used to taking things in life as they came – "whit's fur ye will no go by ye" – he remembered his mother saying, but he felt ill-prepared to deal with this sort of situation. He had a growing conviction that there was something ominous in this coincidence, and for the first time in long enough he realised that he wanted to talk to someone.

Because he had been living in the bothy for some time, the man was known in the village and, whether on his bike or with his dog, he would exchange greetings with the people he met. Conversations, however, were rare, and usually limited to comments about the weather, or some local event or other.

At his place of work, in the local quarry, he kept himself very much to himself. This was easy to do, since the machine he operated was at the rock face in an isolated area, and the noise made any kind of conversation difficult. There was, though, one employee, a local man by the name of Jock Martin, with whom he shared the workshop at lunch time. The man acknowledged that he was really the only person he could confide in – but confide what exactly? After all, what did it amount to really? He had found a stone with letters – a B and another one he couldn't identify – on it; he had felt uncomfortable the previous evening, but for no tangible reason; and today he had come across a drawing that in his own mind he had connected to the stone. But there could well be no relation between any of it, nothing to link them together.

He began to question if it would serve any purpose to talk about such vague matters. Yet he also knew that the more he thought about a course of action, the less likely he was to follow it. He was that sort of person, always

THE STONE OF THE SIDLAWS

finding reasons for not doing something even if it seemed the sensible thing to do. Sometimes he ended up regretting this internal paralysis, sometimes time passed and took care of the matter. Today, however, his misgivings clung to him like misty tendrils on a mountain slope, and nothing seemed able to blow them away.

He felt suddenly tired. He doubted this was because of his exertions of the morning; rather he blamed the turmoil of thoughts in his head. I'll have to sleep on all of this, he decided. If I feel the same tomorrow, I'll speak to Jock.

As he walked to work the next day, he felt relieved of much of the burden of the weekend. His worries had largely dissipated, helped by a good night's sleep and a dose, as he saw it, of common sense. He had been too impressionable, he thought. Maybe he should get out more, meet people, enter into the life of the village.

He walked through the quarry yard, said hello to one of the drivers, who gave him a look, and went into the workshop. Jock's flask and piece-box were sitting on the table, and the man placed his knapsack alongside. The morning passed in the usual racket of crushers, shattered rock, conveyors and trucks. At midday he made his way to the workshop.

"Well Thomas," said Jock as he came in, "Good weekend?"

"All right. Bit of walking with the dog."

"Indeed. I hear you've got started on your renovations."

"Oh?"

"Aye, someone said they saw you doing some measuring yesterday. There's nae secrets around this place!"

Something in his tone made the man start.

"Jock," he asked, "do you know much about the bothy where I live?"

"Och, it's been there for donkey's ages. There's been a few people have bided there over the years."

"Anyone in particular?"

Jock was silent for a moment.

"I mind my faither telling me aboot a foreigner, a Polish chap, who came to stay in it near the end of the war. He'd been in the Free Polish army or something. Anyway, he stayed on after the war. My faither thought he was pretty decent, considering."

"How do you mean?"

"Well, he wasn't the brightest spark, but he was helpful, did odd jobs for the locals. They took a shine to him, even though he never really got the hang of the language. And he was a hardy fellow. In those days there was no water in the bothy. You had to go outside to a spigot, and of course the water was always freezing cauld. My faither minds o' seeing the chiel having a shower at the spigot summer and winter!"

"What happened to him?" asked Thomas. Jock hesitated.

"It was a bit sad really. The chap liked to go walking. The King's Seat was a favourite. Faither often saw him heading off from the bothy, and one day he asked him why he liked going into the hills so often. He said he got a good view of Dundee from up there. He'd look over to the Tay and imagine he was getting on a boat and sailing to Gdansk or whatever."

"Homesick then."

"I suppose so", said Jock. "But here's the thing. One day he didn't come back to the bothy. After a couple of days folk began to wonder what had happened to him. Some of the auld yins began muttering about evil spirits and the like."

"What do you mean, evil?" asked Thomas.

"There's all sorts of legends round here. Mainly about Dunsinnan and its devils. It's all nonsense. Anyway, eventually faither and twa other lads set off to find him. And they did."

"Where was he?"

"Lying on the slopes beneath the King's Seat. Cauld and dead. The doctor said he'd probably had a heart attack up on the hill. Sad, really"

Thomas needed to know more. "Where is he buried?"

"Nobody knows. His body was taken to Dundee, and that's the last anybody heard." Jock paused. "But that's not quite the end of the story."

"No?" Thomas's unease had been returning as Jock's story unfolded.

"People in the village missed him, and someone suggested there should be something to remember him by. So there was a collection, and Andra the mason made a memorial stone and inscribed it. It was taken up the hill and placed where he had been found."

Thomas was aware of his heart beating.

"I think I may have come across the stone."

"That's surprising," said Jock. "It must be very overgrown by now."

THE STONE OF THE SIDLAWS

"What was his name?" asked Thomas.

Jock thought for a moment. "Well, a Polish one obviously. Wilzius or something. Folk just called him Billy, it was easier that way. The name stuck. He even called himself Billy."

Thomas breathed deeply.

"I'm sure it's the same stone." He described where he had found it, and the shape. Jock nodded.

"And the side with the B pointed towards Dundee," Thomas said. He paused, then added, "I suppose the letter on the other side stood for his surname."

Jock looked at him.

"People in the village found his first name difficult enough. They didn't even get to know his second name."

Thomas waited, his heart now hammering in his chest.

"No," continued Jock, "the other side of the stone was left blank."

As Thomas entered the bothy, Kirstie ran towards him and jumped up at him. Thomas pushed her aside, and sat down. He knew he had to do something, and he could think of only one action that might stifle his rising panic.

The pair left the bothy and began to climb uphill. Thomas was heading for the lowest part of the ridge between Black Hill and the King's Seat. The lack of conversation didn't seem to affect Kirstie, who ran and jumped as usual. But in the event it was Kirstie who first alerted him to the proximity of the stone. Suddenly she stopped, her tail went down, she began to bark then whine as if in pain. He looked across the slope, and there it was, more visible this time, he thought, than when he had first seen it.

The wind had risen, gusting across the hill. The heather bent and swayed in its path. Kirstie had lain down, body tense and head twitching. Steeling himself, Thomas slowly approached the stone. Yes, some of the grass had been removed. He was looking at the stone from downhill, and as he got closer, he saw the B. "That's definitely it," he said out loud. He moved round to look at the other side, and stopped in his tracks. There was no lichen, no moss clinging to this side. He stared at the smooth, clean surface. The wind, moaning and shrieking around him, drowned the now-frenzied barking of the dog. He clutched at his chest, and, as he fell to the ground, he saw, etched into the stone, deep and clear, the letter T.

CONTRIBUTORS' NOTES

Amanda Barclay *Through A Glass Darkly* – **Methil Power Station**

I have a strange fondness for Methil Power station. It has been a distinctive East Fife landmark for all my life. The plant closed in 2000 and now cuts a forlorn figure as it awaits demolition. I was keen to set a story there to mark its passing. Whilst the exterior of the building is as familiar as my own hand, I wanted to find out more about the interior. In doing so I discovered the covert but fascinating world of urban exploration. This is my third outing with Nethergate Writers.

Beth Blackmore *The Saving O' Murdie Boon* – **Dundee (and Perthshire)**

Far from the backcourts of late 19th Century Dundee, a rough stone road went wandering up the sloping fields of the Angus Howe. It was this harsh and lonely setting that inspired me to write a short story about two unlikely lads forced to leave 'the toun' and flee together to where the high hills glowered down on the 'lang rigs and haystooks'. I have attempted to write 'in the speak' of the old, broad Scots, including an earthy mixture of dialects and tradition.

David Carson *The Stone of the Sidlaws* – **The Sidlaw Hills**

The Sidlaws are prominent in the views from where I stay. It was a while before I walked in them, however – bigger hills had a greater attraction. When my children expressed interest in hillwalking, the Sidlaws seemed a good place to start (and our dog came too). Over the years, they have proved very rewarding. They offer short and longer walks, views out of all proportion to their height, and are usually empty.

There really is a stone, not dissimilar to the one in the story, but, so far at least, it has displayed none of the malevolent characteristics of its fictional counterpart!

CONTRIBUTORS' NOTES

Flora Davidson *Dilemma* – Glen Clova

I start with a character and put her (it's usually a her) in a situation that brings out her idiosyncracies. In 'Dilemma' a sublime wild place infects an old-fashioned academic's rectitude with rapture. Her self-discipline, struggling to hold the front, calls in dubious allies. It's only in this class I've found one does not need a hundred thousand words to tell a story, nor spell out each quirk of character over a stretch of years. Just show the revealing moment.

Bob Drysdale *The Battle of South Esk* – Montrose

I have always had a great interest in the Jacobite rebellions and I came across this story some time ago. I know the town of Montrose fairly well and I thought it would be interesting to retell a forgotten episode in its history. The people named in the story were mostly real townspeople of the time and the Auchterlonys and William Cargill are recorded as prisoners after Culloden. William Cargill was eventually sentenced to transportation to Virginia.

The sloop *Hazard* after her capture was taken into the service of the Jacobites and renamed *Le Prince Charles*. She was crewed by the men from the French ship which was run aground in the harbour. She was eventually recaptured when she returned to Scottish waters in April 1746 with gold and arms for the Jacobites.

Pat Fox *Release- Glenfarg* – Glenfarg

'Release' is a description of something that appeared to happen. For a while I believed that it did indeed happen but now I know it did not. So I am still pursuing the sound of complete silence – and this poem is untrue!

Lesley Holmes *A Walk in the Park* – Baxter Park

Baxter Park is a dominant feature of Stobswell, and in my own life, as a place of relaxation, exercise and a short cut on my many walks into Dundee. I've followed the park's recent regeneration to its former Victorian glory, in particular, the Renaissance Pavilion centrepiece, now designated a civil marriage venue. This inspired, 'A Walk in the Park', the story of a middle aged man arranging the renewal of wedding vows as a surprise for his wife. I also greatly enjoy fiction with a supernatural twist, and had great fun including a cat that morphs into a young vandal to test the integrity of these visitors to the park.

Jean Langlands *Digging In* – South Angus

I was born and brought up in Glasgow but knew from an early age that I wanted to live in the country. My wish came true in 1976 when my husband and I moved to the county of Angus. I have spent the last thirty years or so exploring the area and observing every aspect of the countryside I love and the people in it. It occurred to me that a person could be so deeply rooted in an area (town or country) as to be almost a part of it. And thus began the idea for my story about a woman who, in spite of her advancing years, refuses to give up her way of life.

Ward McGaughrin *Scratching The Surface* – The Howff

As a new writer I've learned the truth in the phrase, "Nothing good is ever written, only re-written". I've accumulated more experience from every single re-write and I'm sure lots more lie ahead. I chose The Howff as a setting because it's a place I know well both as a shortcut and a photographic location. The story came from one of those "What if ..." ideas.

Roddie McKenzie *Sinderin* – Pitmiddle

My story 'Sinderin' is set in the deserted village of Pitmiddle, Perthshire. I came across the legend "Deserted Village" while looking over an Ordnance Survey map of the Braes of the Carse and was intrigued. A trip up there in autumn revealed the fantastic views from the site and I could make out the the position of the walls of most of the houses. Some of the houses still had artefacts lying in them, which gave a human presence and poignancy to the location. I researched Pitmiddle and thought that it was a good example of how long-established close communities could be destroyed by landlord policies. I felt it necessary for this to be remembered, which led me to write 'Sinderin'.

CONTRIBUTORS' NOTES

End of the Line *by Joyce McKinney* **– Elie**

I started writing because my children were constantly asking about places we had been to and things we had done before they were all around. Now we are retired and living in a beautiful part of Fife. People are inspired to draw and paint here. The small villages abound with colourful characters and the population changes with the seasons. I have more opportunity to read, which occupies a great deal of my time, and I would love to learn to write as well as some of the authors I admire.

Claire MacLeary *Nora's Garden* **– St. Andrews**

Originally from Glasgow, I pursued an early career as a Personnel Manager and Training Consultant. I have lived in Fife for the past twenty years, running a variety of businesses in St Andrews, world renowned as the home of golf. The town's historic landmarks are well-publicised, but it is the hidden St. Andrews – the quirky homes and secret gardens to be discovered down its narrow lanes – which inspired my story *Nora's Garden*.

John Mooney *The Ringo Kid* **– North Wellington Street, Dundee**

The location I chose is where I lived until I was eleven years old. I still have vivid memories of the various "lands" that made up the tenements and the people who lived there. But my clearest memory of this period, and this is where the story comes from, is of how important a part the cinema played in our lives. In the story John says he never shot anyone in the back because Ringo wouldn't have done that. The films gave us a moral code and we followed it. John Wayne would never hit anyone with glasses, the cavalry would always appear at the last minute to save us, the good guys wore white hats and always won and the bad guys were usually dressed in black. Sixty years on, and I still find myself looking for the cavalry.

Jane O'Neill *The Winkle Seller* **– Grassy Beach, Broughty Ferry**

Grassy Beach is the setting for this, my first poem. Linked by footpaths from Broughty Ferry to The Stannergate, it was a favourite beauty spot in the 50s and

CONTRIBUTORS' NOTES

is one of the few original grasslands left in Dundee. With its beach of smooth stones and dusty grass this strip of foreshore attracted not only striking black and white oystercatchers wading for food at low tide, but winkle collectors who could also be seen foraging in the slippy seaweed and rocks. They sold their pickings in the neighbouring housing schemes, usually from a barrow or an old pram. The winkle seller was an alluring visitor and children did follow him as though he was the Pied Piper! But as the child in my poem finds out, her boldness leads to an unexpected outcome.

Ann Prescott – *Monkey Tricks* Botanic Gardens, Dundee

Despite the perils of planners and the greed of developers the University of Dundee's Botanic Gardens continue to lead a charmed existence as the most magical place in the city. This magic is what I've tried to capture in my story. I am indebted to my nephew, Mark, for his translation of the Utterance.

Louise Ramsay *The White Snake of Reekie Linn* – Reekie Linn waterfall

I have lived at Bamff, near Alyth, for nearly thirty years. Bamff is about three miles from the Reekie Linn. That is perhaps why this spectacular waterfall features in the origin myth of the Ramsay family who have held Bamff for 777 years this year. Generations of Ramsays, including our four children, were brought up on this story. Once, we climbed down the bank and swam in the pool and explored Neis's cave. Here, I have treated the myth – in which historical facts have been threaded together with a Celtic folk tale – as though it were all true.

George Reid *The Bench* – Dunfermline

I was born in Dunfermline and attended the old Commercial Primary School in East Port. I passed the public park on my way to and from school every day and played there with my friends during the school holidays. I walked through the park last October for the first time in about thirty years and through my observations I found the inspiration for my contribution to *If Stones Could Speak*.

CONTRIBUTORS' NOTES

Nan Rice *Right Time, Right Place* **– Dundee City Centre**

A retired Police Officer, I came to 'bide' in Dundee in 1985. After Glasgow, I revelled in the 'county town' atmosphere, the sight of well groomed ladies congregating in Keillor's Tearoom in the High Street for morning coffee, the beautiful architecture in the town centre, and the keen sense of history. For *If Stones Could Speak*, I decided to become my character, Detective Sergeant Charlie Mahoney, and weave my story around Dundee. Although restricted in my choice of places to mention, I hope Charlie was able to convey the pride he felt in the town's history.

Faye Stevenson *Vantage Point* **– Falkland Hill**

I can see Falkland Hill from my front door. A brisk walk takes me to the bottom in twenty minutes. On lazier days, I park halfway up and climb the rest. Locals say that if you can't see the top it must be raining. If you can see it, then it's about to rain! Researching for 'Vantage Point' gave me the opportunity to explore my journeys to the top with fresh, objective eyes. The idea for the story came to me when my daughter's boyfriend had his car broken into on Boxing Day whilst hill walking.

Paul Sykes *The Challenge* **– Cupar and Tarvit Hill Golf Club**

I wanted to write a humorous piece where I could bring two, at first fairly unlikeable characters together in a conflict that reveals a more human side to each of them. I chose the location because I know Tarvit Hill and the House very well. My son and I go sledging there nearly every year! I thought that the old-style hickory golf would add to the humour as well as give a flavour of the place. Since I started writing this piece the National Trust in their finite wisdom have decided to close Tarvit House. So the fight starts here!

Ed Thompson *Mr. Stanley, I Presume?* **– West End, Dundee**

The narrow pends and wynds of Dundee – Couttie's Wynd, Rankine's Court, Mary Ann Lane, for example – are shabby reminders of the shape of a city now largely lost. I chose the lane beside the Speedwell in Perth Road as the setting for my story, because I was told many years ago that it was a portal into the 'West End Triangle', an area where people might disappear for hours on end; when they reappeared they were unsteady on their feet and strangely unintelligible in their speech.

Stuart Wardrop *Cast Adrift* – North Queensferry

I like writing about what goes on in the heads of characters – especially flawed ones like Duggie. I still visit North Queensferry and have fond, if perhaps idealised, childhood memories of everything and everyone I associate with it. So for me, using the Ferry as backdrop to a story featuring the less than perfect Duggie was as natural as pulling on old and comfortable boots. I close my eyes and see where he parked, I hear the same trains echoing on the bridge, I smell salty seaweed and I well remember chucking-out time at the Albert.

Catherine Young *Blue Skies* – St Cyrus

My childhood home was encircled by hills. I vividly recall the moment – during a seaside holiday when I was five – when I realised the world didn't have *sides* and that *the sky came right down to the ground*. I was reminded of that excitement on my first trip to St Cyrus's stunning coastal cliffs ten years ago. In 'Blue Skies' I hope to convey the sense of endless possibilities that these vast skies and limitless horizons evoke for me. I have had stories published in local anthologies and selected for *Winter Words*, 2007. I am currently working on more short stories.

UNIVERSITY OF DUNDEE

Continuing Education Courses for Adults

A wide range of short day time classes, evening courses and Saturday workshops are available to the public at the University of Dundee including

- Art & Design
- Art History
- Astronomy
- Behavioural Studies
- Business Skills
- Child Development
- Counselling
- Creative Writing
- Film & Media
- History
- Horticulture
- Human Relations
- Law
- Literature
- Music & Performing Arts
- Personal Development
- Philosophy & Religion
- Poetry
- Reiki
- Science & Nature
- Social Studies
- Song Writing

Courses also run in Perth and Angus.
For further information and enrolments contact

Continuing Education
Tower Building
University of Dundee
Nethergate
Dundee DD1 4HN

01382 384809/384128
conted@dundee.ac.uk
www.dundee.ac.uk/conted